STERI
Test Prep

LAW ESSENTIALS

Real Property

Governing Law

3rd edition

3   2   1

ISBN-13: 978-1-9547251-1-9

Sterling Test Prep products are available at quantity discounts.

For more information, contact info@sterling–prep.com.

Sterling Test Prep
6 Liberty Square #11
Boston, MA 02109

©2022 Sterling Test Prep
Published by Sterling Test Prep
Printed in the U.S.A.

Customer Satisfaction Guarantee

Your feedback is important because we strive to provide the highest quality prep materials. Email us comments or suggestions.

info@sterling–prep.com

We reply to emails – check your spam folder

Thank you for choosing our book!

STERLING
Test Prep

Thousands of students use our study aids to prepare for law school exams and to pass the bar!

Passing the bar is essential for admission to practice law and launching your legal career.

This preparation guide describes the principles of substantive law governing the correct answers to exam questions. It was developed by legal professionals and law instructors who possess extensive credentials and have been admitted to practice law in several jurisdictions. The content is clearly presented and systematically organized for targeted preparation.

The performance on individual questions has been correlated with success or failure on the bar. By analyzing previously administered exams, the authors identified these predictive items and assembled the rules of law that govern the answers to questions tested. Learn the essential governing law to make fine-line distinctions among related principles and decide between tough choices on the exam. This knowledge is vital to excel in law school finals and pass the bar exam.

We look forward to being an essential part of your preparation and wish you great success in the legal profession!

210630vgr

Law Essentials series

Constitutional Law	Criminal Law and Criminal Procedure
Contracts	Business Associations
Evidence	Conflict of Laws
Real Property	Family Law
Torts	Secured Transactions
Civil Procedure	Trusts and Estates

Visit our Amazon store

Comprehensive Glossary of Legal Terms

Over 2,100 essential legal terms defined and explained. An excellent reference source for law students, practitioners and readers seeking an understanding of legal vocabulary and its application.

Landmark U.S. Supreme Court Cases: Essential Summaries

Learn important constitutional cases that shaped American law. Understand how the evolving needs of society intersect with the U.S. Constitution. Short summaries of seminal Supreme Court cases focused on issues and holdings.

Visit our Amazon store

Table of Contents

REAL PROPERTY GOVERNING LAW (*continued*)

REAL PROPERTY GOVERNING LAW (*continued*)

EXAM INFORMATION, PREP & TEST-TAKING STRATEGIES (*continued*)

EXAM INFORMATION, PREP & TEST-TAKING STRATEGIES (*continued*)

APPENDIX (*continued*)

Real Property Governing Law

On the MEE, Real Property is tested about every other cycle and generally is not combined with other topics. Real Property is a difficult subject, so focus on the highly tested issues: real estate contracts and deeds, ownership and title to property, recording acts, mortgages and security devices, leases, and rights in land. Know the essential terminology such as mortgagor, mortgagee, warranty deed, quitclaim deed, wild deed, assignment, joint tenancy, sublease, easement, merger, equitable conversion, and adverse possession.

The statements herein were compiled by analyzing released Real Property questions and setting forth the principles of law governing the correct answers. Review these principles before preparing answers to practice Real Property questions. Memorize this governing law and understand how it applies to the correct answer.

STERLING
Test Prep

Real Property Law – Overview

Personal Property: goods or chattels that are not real property

Tangible property: physically defined property, such as goods, animals, and minerals

Intangible property: represents rights not reduced to physical forms (e.g., stock certificates).

Choice of categories

At common law, found property is categorized in five ways:

> *Abandoned property* – the owner has discarded or voluntarily forsaken to terminate their ownership without vesting ownership in another.

> *Lost property* – the owner has involuntarily and unintentionally parted with it through neglect or carelessness and does not know its location.

> *Mislaid property* – the owner has intentionally set it down to retrieve it and forget where they put it.

> *Treasure trove* – a category exclusively for gold or silver in coin, plate, bullion, or paper money equivalents, found concealed in the earth, a building, or another private place. Treasure trove carries thoughts of antiquity (i.e., the treasure has been concealed for so long as to indicate that the owner is probably dead or unknown).

> *Embedded property* – personal property that has become part of the natural earth. Examples include pottery, the sunken wreck of a steamship, or a sack of precious gems buried in the ground). Possession of embedded property goes to the owner of the land on which the property was found.

Under these doctrines, the finder of lost property, abandoned property, and treasure trove acquires a right to possess the property against the entire world, except the rightful owner, regardless of the place of finding.

The finder of mislaid property is required to turn it over to the owner of the premises, who has a duty to safeguard the property for the true owner.

One of the major distinctions between these categories is that only lost property necessarily involves an element of involuntariness.

The four remaining categories involve voluntary and intentional acts by the owner in placing the property where another eventually finds it.

Despite not being lost or abandoned property, the treasure trove has the right to possession recognized to be in the finder rather than the premises' owner.

Law of finders for personal property

Personal property can be abandoned, lost or mislaid

Abandoned property

The true owner has voluntarily given up claims of ownership

Lost or mislaid property

Lost property has an unknown location

Mislaid property is when the true owner placed somewhere, intending to return, but which could not be located

General rule

A finder of abandoned property acquires title

General rule

A finder's title is good against others except the true owner, prior finders and some landowners

Finder *vs.* true owner

The finder has rights more than others, except the true owner

Finder *vs.* landowner

Generally, the owner of the land prevails over the finder

Finder *vs.* prior finder

Prior finders prevail to encourage finders to use instead of hiding it

Trespassing finders

Trespassing finders of lost or mislaid property lose

Employee finders

Old: found property belongs to the employer

Modern: finder prevails (for public policy)

Invitee finders

Property found during invited purpose must be surrendered to landowner

Embedded object

Property embedded in soil must be returned to the landowner, but if it is on top of soil, finder may prevail

Private places

Homeowners awarded objects found in their home unless absentee owners – no constant possession

Public places

Lost property goes to finder since restoring it to the true owner is unlikely

Mislaid: goes to landowner

The Estate System

Fee simple

A conveyance from owner to "A" or to "A and their heirs" creates a fee simple interest in A and no interest in A's heirs.

Fee simple determinable

A fee simple determinable is created by a conveyance that limits the fee by the grant's words such as "so long as."

The grantor's interest following a fee simple determinable is a possibility of reverter, a reversionary interest not subject to the rule against perpetuities.

In the case of a fee simple determinable, when and if the event is a limitation on the fee occurs, the present interest holder's interest is automatically terminated. The title goes to the grantor as the holder of the future interest.

A right given to a third person after the termination of a fee simple determinable (to A, so long as the premises are used for church premises and if they are not so used, then to B) creates an executory interest in B, which is subject to the rule against perpetuities.

That executory interest is invalid unless any right in the third party must occur within the period of the rule (lives in being plus 21 years) if it will ever occur.

If an invalid executory interest fails, the grantor takes it because they retain the possibility of reverter.

Fee simple subject to condition subsequent

A fee simple subject to condition subsequent is created by a conveyance which grants a fee simple interest and then terminates it if a contingency occurs, usually with the words "but if."

The grantor's reversionary type interest is called a "right of entry for condition broken" and is not subject to the rule against perpetuities.

If the right of entry is given to a person other than the grantor, that right is an executory interest subject to the rule against perpetuities.

If the executory interest is invalid after a right of entry for a condition broken, the grantor takes nothing, and the grantee holds in fee simple.

A fee simple determinable or a fee simple subject to a condition subsequent are the only devices that will allow a seller who retains no land in the vicinity of the property conveyed to control the property's use.

While the possibility of reverter becomes possessory automatically upon the breach of the condition, a person holding a right of entry for condition broken must bring a court proceeding to enforce that right before obtaining ownership.

Future interests

A *reversion* is a future interest in the grantor, consisting of any interest that does not convey.

A reversion is considered vested and is not subject to the rule against perpetuities.

A *remainder* is a future interest created in a party other than the grantor in the same instrument as the prior possessory interest and capable of taking effect at the prior interest termination.

A remainder is vested if it is ready to take in possession whenever the previous possessory interest terminates.

For example, in conveyance "to A for life and then to B," the remainder is vested because either B or B's heirs or devisees own the property upon the termination of the life estate in A.

A remainder is contingent if a condition precedent must be satisfied before the interest becomes possessory.

For example, in the conveyance to "A for life and then to B if B survives A," neither the remainderman, B, nor heirs take if B predeceases A.

A remainder is contingent if the holders of the interest, such as heirs of a living person or unborn children, are unascertained.

A *contingent remainder* becomes vested once the condition precedent is satisfied, or the indefinite beneficiaries (e.g., heirs of a living person) become identified when that person dies.

If a fee simple interest is conveyed subject to a condition precedent, title and possession remain in the grantor.

The grantee does not take until the condition precedent has been satisfied.

While a remainder interest to the "children of A, a living person" is contingent if A has no children, interest is classified as vested subject to open if A already has one or more children.

The interests of the existing children are reduced as the class expands to include afterborn children of A.

The grantee of a contingent remainder takes nothing if the condition precedent is never satisfied.

An executory interest is an interest in land to a third person after a fee simple subject to divestment.

If an interest in land is a contingent remainder and cannot become possessory immediately upon termination of the prior estate because the condition precedent has not been satisfied, the interest is transformed into an executory interest, which will take possession when the condition precedent to its taking is satisfied.

In the meantime, there is a reversion in the grantor.

Class gifts

If there is a class gift, one to individuals bearing a family relationship to a named individual, such as the "grandchildren of A," afterborn members of the class can join the class until the class closes.

If the grantor does not indicate otherwise, the class closes when any member of the class can take possession of the gift.

For example, if the gift is "to my grandchildren when they reach age 21," the class closes when the first grandchild is eligible to take the interest by reaching age 21.

A future interest, whether vested or contingent, can be alienated before its becoming possessory.

Notes for active learning

Life estates

At the termination of a life estate's measuring life, the property reverts to the grantor unless the grantor has deeded a remainder interest after the life estate, title vests in the remainderman.

A life estate that is limited by an event such as remarriage is a determinable life estate and terminates either on the holder's death or upon the event's happening, whichever occurs sooner.

Waste is an action of the life tenant, which reduces the value of a future interest in the property.

If the life tenant takes an action that increases the value of the remainder, that action is ameliorating waste, and the life tenant is not liable for destruction, which occurs in the process of increasing value.

Vested and contingent remaindermen have standing to enjoin a life tenant from committing waste.

The holder of a possibility of reverter, a right of entry for condition subsequent, or an executory interest after a fee simple subject to a condition subsequent does not.

When a mineral extraction activity had commenced before the property was divided between a life tenancy and a remainder interest, the life tenant can continue that extraction activity without being liable for waste without having to account to the remainderman.

If a person holds a life estate *pur autre vie*, the measuring life is a person other than the holder of the possessory interest. The estate terminates at the death of the person who is the measuring life, not upon the death of the person in possession.

When a grantor conveys property subject to a mortgage to a life tenant and remainderman, the life tenant must pay the interest on the mortgage and current real estate taxes if the property generates income sufficient to make such payments, and the remainderman must make principal payments.

Neither life tenant nor remainderman is personally liable on the mortgage note.

If the property generates no income, the life tenant is not personally liable to the remainderman for interest and taxes paid by them.

If the grantor deeds a life estate to a grantee, the grantee's life is the measuring life.

If the grantee sells their life estate, the grantee's life, not the purchaser's life, remains the measuring life.

The rule against perpetuities (RAP)

The common-law rule against perpetuities (RAP) provides that no interest in land is valid unless it must vest, if it ever vests, within 21 years of lives in being at the creation of the interest.

The rule against perpetuities does not apply to reversions retained by the grantor and reversionary type interests such as reverter and rights of entry for conditions subsequent, or to the grantee who holds such a reversionary interest because of a conveyance from the grantor.

The rule against perpetuities does apply to future interests created in persons other than the grantor.

Those interests are the remainder, executory interests, and first refusal rights.

The validity of the interest to which the rule against perpetuities applies depends on whether the interest must vest, or in some circumstances, must become possessory within the statutory period set by the rule.

The first issue in determining the validity of interest is when the period established by the rule starts to run.

If a will creates an interest in land, the period starts to run at the testator's death. Individuals alive at that time are eligible to be measuring lives.

If an *inter vivos* conveyance creates an interest in land, the period starts to run at the time of conveyance. Individuals alive at that time are eligible to be measuring lives.

If an *inter vivos* conveyance creates the interest in land to trust, and if the trust is irrevocable, the period starts to run at the time of the conveyance.

If the trust is initially revocable, the period starts to run when the power to amend or revoke the trust is terminated through the death of the person with the power to amend or terminate it or the relinquishment of the power thereof.

A child conceived but not born at the time of the commencement of the rule will be considered a life in being.

Thus, if a father dies before his child is born, that child will be considered a life in being at the father's death.

The period during which interest must vest under the rule is a minimum of 21 years from when the period begins to run.

That period is extended by the lives in being at the time of the creation of the interest so that the maximum period for vesting is extended to 21 years after the death of a life in being at the creation of the interest, otherwise known as a measuring life.

An interest vests when all persons taking the interest have been ascertained, and no condition precedent prevents their interest from becoming possessory whenever the preceding interest terminates.

If an interest must vest within 21 years when the rule starts to run, it is valid without considering any measuring lives that might extend the period during which the rule runs.

The 21-year period does not make it so that persons born within 21 years of the time that the running of the rule commences constituting measuring lives.

Remainders that may remain contingent beyond the period of the rule, executory interests that may not become possessory during the period, and rights of first refusal that may not become operative during the rule are invalid because of the rule against perpetuities.

Under the common-law rule against perpetuities, a person's ability to have children until death is irrebuttable. If the presence of that possibility prevents an interest from becoming vested during the period of the rule, that interest is invalid.

Under the common-law rule against perpetuities as applied to class gifts, the entire disposition is invalid if any member of the class's interest is invalid.

When an interest is invalid because of the rule against perpetuities, the following rules determine the construction of the conveyance:

If the conveyance has multiple alternative dispositions and only one is invalid, the disposition is construed with the invalid gift deleted.

If the invalid interest is the will's residuary clause, the testator's heirs take. Those heirs under the modern law are determined as if the testator died when the last valid interest terminated, not at the time of the testator's death.

If a conveyance creates an invalid interest, the grantor or the grantor's heirs take by reversion.

Powers of appointment

A power of appointment permits the holder of the power either during that holder's lifetime or in the holder's will to direct the disposition of assets set up in trust by the grantor of that trust containing the power.

A power of appointment is special if the potential beneficiaries of the exercise of that power are limited and general if the holder of the power can direct the assets to anyone.

Jurisdictions are split on whether a will's residuary clause, which does not explicitly refer to a general power of appointment, exercises that power in favor of the residuary beneficiary.

The period of the rule against perpetuities does not start to run until the holder's power of appointment is either exercised or expires.

The period for the rule against perpetuities for a special power of appointment starts to run when the trust becomes irrevocable.

Restraints on alienation

A right reserved by the seller to repurchase the property at the same price, which the owner could obtain from a third party, a right of first refusal, is not an invalid restraint on alienation.

If such a right can be exercised in a time which extends beyond the operative time for the rule against perpetuities, it is invalid, even during the fixed 21-year period of the rule.

A prohibition in a conveyance by the grantor of a grantee's right to alienate property or a provision forfeiting an interest if the grantee attempts to alienate property is invalid.

If an owner of property enters into a contract restricting their right to alienate property, that contract is valid.

Restraints on alienation are invalid only when imposed on the grantee of property by the grantor.

Characteristics of co-tenancies

There is no right of survivorship when parties own property as tenants in common.

Joint tenancy is not devisable or inheritable and cannot be severed by a will.

A co-tenant who makes improvements to the property cannot charge co-tenants for contribution to the cost of the improvements. However, those improvements can be considered in a partition proceeding.

When the property is partitioned, it is accompanied by an accounting between co-tenants concerning payments of expenses and collection of rents.

A co-tenant occupying the property they own as a co-tenant does not owe rent to co-tenants.

Co-tenants holding as joint tenants or tenants in common have an inalienable right to partition.

A tenancy by the entirety can be partitioned by joint deeds of the two co-owners or if the entirety is converted to a tenancy in common by divorce.

The preferred method of partition is a physical division of the property.

When a physical division is not feasible or cannot be accomplished so that each party is fairly treated, the partition is accomplished by a sale at auction and a division of the proceeds.

When parties hold property in joint tenancy or tenancy by the entirety, one tenant's death triggers the complete title vesting in the surviving tenant.

Furthermore, an involuntary lien placed against the interest of the dead co-tenant does not burden the surviving co-tenant.

If one joint owner mortgages their interest in the property and later dies, the interest passes to the other joint tenant free of the mortgage.

One tenant in common owes a fiduciary duty to permit the other co-tenant to maintain proportionate property ownership by paying their proportionate share of debt if one co-tenant acquires the property at a foreclosure sale.

Co-tenancy between spouses

A tenancy by the entirety can only be created between spouses.

Neither party can terminate the tenancy by the entirety using a unilateral act during the marriage.

If one spouse attempts to convey their interest, the conveyance is void, and the spouses still hold the title as tenants by the entirety.

If two persons who are not married take title as tenants by the entirety, they hold the title as joint tenants.

Conversion of joint tenancies into tenancies in common

One joint tenant's conveyance of their interest to a third party converts the title to tenancy in common rights between the other original joint tenant and the third-party grantee.

The joint tenancy is terminated even if the third party reconveys to the original joint tenant.

If a mortgage on the property only creates a lien under state law, one joint tenant granting a mortgage does not terminate the joint tenancy.

If granting a mortgage under state law vests title in the mortgagee subject to a right of redemption, granting a mortgage by one joint tenant terminates the *joint tenancy* and transforms it into a *tenancy in common* between the original joint tenants.

Two joint tenants' simultaneous death creates an undivided one-half interest as a tenant in common in each joint tenant's estates.

If A and B, who hold the entire fee in a parcel of land, jointly convey an undivided one-third interest in the property to C, A and B still hold an undivided two-thirds interest as joint tenants, not as tenants in common. C holds their interest as a *tenant in common* with A and B.

Rights and liabilities of adjoining landowners

The owner of land in its natural state can successfully sue an adjoining landowner who disturbs the support that the adjoining land provides on a strict liability theory without showing negligence.

The owner of improved land can successfully sue an adjoining landowner who disturbs that support only if they prove that the adjoining landowner is negligent.

Rights in Land

Express easements

An *express easement*, or easement by grant, must be in writing and signed by the grantor of the burdened land to be valid.

If permission is oral by the landowner to use land, a license, not an easement, is created.

The *license* is terminable at the will of the owner of the land.

Express easements are interests in land subject to the recording system.

An easement by a grant must be recorded to burden *bona fide* purchasers of the burdened (i.e., servient) land.

An express easement is subject to superior rights existing on the servient estate when it is recorded.

If a mortgage on the property is foreclosed, the purchaser at the foreclosure sale is not burdened by the easement.

An easement is appurtenant if it burdens one parcel of land, the servient estate, for another parcel's specific benefit, the dominant estate.

A conveyance of a parcel of land, which has the benefit of an appurtenant easement, automatically transfers to the grantee the rights in that appurtenant easement even if it is not mentioned in the conveyance.

If the benefits of an easement are appurtenant to one parcel of land, the owner of that land cannot use the easement to benefit an adjacent parcel they own.

The easement is deemed to be "overburdened."

A holder of an appurtenant easement can only transfer the benefits of that easement by transferring the ownership interest in the benefited estate.

An attempted alienation of the easement rights to a person who does not own the benefited estate destroys the easement.

The holder of an easement has the right to make repairs to property within the easement they have a right to use (e.g., stairs, pipes, roads) but does not have an obligation to repair unless they agree.

A person cannot have an easement on land which they own in fee simple.

If the benefited estate holder acquires the servient estate fee simple, the easement is destroyed by merger.

If the two estates are separated later, the deed to the dominant estate creates an easement over the servient estate only if the easement right is expressly granted in the deed.

This principle is not applicable unless the holder has identical interests in the dominant and servient estates.

Even though an oral agreement will not create an easement, if a landowner induces a neighboring landowner to substantially rely on them not assert their property right, the owner is estopped asserting property rights they said would be waived.

Overuse of an easement can be prohibited by an injunction but does not destroy the easement.

When the exact location of an easement is not specified, the servient estate owner has the right to reasonably locate the precise right-of-way.

Once the right-of-way location is established, the easement's location becomes fixed and cannot be moved without the owners of the servient and dominant estates' consent.

An express easement can be terminated by adverse possession if the landowner affirmatively bars the easement holder from using the easement for the statutory period.

Failure to use an easement right, by itself, is insufficient to terminate an easement.

An express easement is valid for an indefinite time unless its duration is limited in the grant itself or subsequently limited in time by the dominant estate holder.

The end of the reason for creating an express easement does not terminate an express easement.

Profit-a-prendre

A *profit-a-prendre* (French, *right of taking*) combines an easement right to enter the land of another and the right to sever interests (e.g., timber, minerals) from the land and remove them.

Because a *profit-a-prendre* incorporates an easement right, it is an interest in property that must be created and recorded with the same formalities as an express easement and unlimited in time unless a time limit is specified.

A *profit-a-prendre* can give the holder an exclusive right to sever property from the land so that the land's fee simple owner no longer has that right.

If the holder has an exclusive right, they can divide that right and assign portions to others.

If the *profit-a-prendre* is not exclusive, the holder cannot apportion it.

Easements by necessity and implication

Easements by necessity and implication arise out of the presumed intent of the parties to a conveyance.

If the document states explicitly there is no intent to create an easement right, neither an easement by necessity nor implication will arise.

An easement by necessity arises only where the parcel is being severed by a conveyance of part of a larger parcel is landlocked and has no legal access of any kind.

The easement is an easement by reservation if the grantor is the party retaining the landlocked parcel of land.

An easement by implication (a situation where a *quasi*-easement exists at the time of the separation of the dominant and servient estates) will be created as long as the easement is reasonably necessary to serve the dominant estate.

An easement by necessity or implication arises only when there is no express easement.

An easement by necessity or implication can only be created during the division of a commonly owned parcel.

If a parcel later becomes landlocked because of an eminent domain taking or otherwise, there is no easement over the larger parcel of land from which the landlocked parcel came.

An easement created by necessity ends when the necessity ends.

For example, if the government provided access to a formerly landlocked parcel, the easement by necessity once held over the adjoining land would terminate.

An easement for light and air or view can only be created by an express easement; such an easement does not arise by necessity or implication.

An easement by necessity or implication need not be recorded to be effective against *bona fide* purchasers.

Adverse possession

Title by adverse possession is obtained if the possessor is in continuous, open, and notorious adverse possession and has exclusive possession for the statutory period.

The method of calculating the statutory period is:

> The period for adverse possession does not start to run while the true owner is a minor or is adjudicated mentally incompetent.

> If the adverse possessor initially goes into possession while a competent adult owns the property, the subsequent transfer of ownership to a minor or a person with a disability does not interrupt the running of the statutory period.

> If the true owner transfers title to the property while the adverse possessor is in possession, the running of the statutory period is not interrupted.

> The adverse possessor is entitled to aggregate their time in possession against successive owners to achieve adverse possession for the required statutory period.

> The consensual transfer of possessory rights from one adverse possessor to a subsequent adverse possessor permits the subsequent adverse possessor to include the time in which their predecessor was in possession to achieve adverse possession for the required statutory period.

The requirement of continuous and exclusive possession states that:

> If the true owner possesses the property in common with the adverse possessor at any time during the required statutory period, the adverse possessor is no longer maintaining continuous, exclusive possession and must start the statutory period again once the true owner leaves.

> The actions necessary to satisfy the exclusive and continuous requirements depend upon the type of property involved.

> The requirements are less strict for an uninhabited rural or seasonal property than for urban property.

> Fencing in the adjacent property or placing all or part of a building on the property adjacent to the property owned satisfies the continuous and exclusive requirements.

The requirement that possession be adverse states that:

> Because a co-tenant has a right to occupy all the property they hold as a co-tenant, open, notorious, and exclusive possession by one co-tenant for the statutory period will not establish adverse possession unless explicit notice was given to the other co-tenant at the beginning of that period.

Such notice is usually in the form of a co-tenant barring another from using the property.

Unless it is established that the possession was permissive, possession by an individual where nothing concerning permission is established is considered adverse.

An adverse possessor need not know that they possess the property of another to obtain the property by adverse possession.

Fencing in property belonging to a neighbor in the mistaken belief that the adverse possessor is fencing in their property is sufficient to establish adverse possession.

Title by adverse possession can be obtained to airspace by projections from a structure that overhangs the abutting property.

After an adverse possessor's actions have enabled them to obtain title by adverse possession, the interruption of their exclusive possession by anyone, including the true owner, will not defeat the adverse possessor's title.

Neither title by adverse possession, nor an easement by prescription, need be recorded to be valid against the record titleholder or purchaser.

If two persons act together to obtain title by adverse possession, the adverse possessors hold as tenants in common, not joint tenants.

If one of two adverse possessors dies, their interest in the property goes to their heirs or devisees, not to the surviving joint adverse possessor.

Easements by prescription

The difference between the conduct necessary to achieve an easement by prescription and that needed to obtain title by adverse possession is that possession need not be exclusive to obtain an easement by prescription.

How the property is used during the period necessary to acquire an easement by prescription defines the easement scope after the prescriptive period.

Once the conduct necessary to obtain an easement by prescription continues for the time necessary to achieve the easement, continuous use of the easement after that is not necessary to maintain it.

An easement by prescription can be obtained even if the person acquiring an easement by prescription uses the property without communicating that the use is adverse.

If the use of property commenced as a permissive use, notice to the owner that its character had changed and was adverse would be required to obtain an easement by prescription.

The holder of an easement by prescription has no obligation to keep it in repair.

Fixtures

Upon default, the holder of a properly recorded purchase money security interest can remove a fixture over the objection of a real estate mortgagee if the property subject to the interest is removable, even if the mortgage date preceded the date of the security interest.

A tenant for a fixed term has the right to remove personal property (i.e., trade fixtures) that they attached to the real estate for the lease term, even though the attachment of the property might cause it to be characterized as real property,

A person having an estate of uncertain duration (such as a life estate) who plants crops on that land can enter the land and remove the crops at the end of the growing season even if the possessory property right has terminated.

A person having an estate of uncertain duration who attaches fixtures to the real estate, which can easily be removed without damage to the real estate, can remove them within a reasonable time after the estate terminates.

In a life estate, the personal representative can remove the fixtures.

The mortgagee cannot prevent the mortgagor from removing portions of the real estate secured by their mortgage if removing the structure would leave adequate security for the mortgagee, and removal is reasonable and proper in the prudent management of the business.

Covenants

Covenants run with the land and bind successor owners if:

- they are in writing and formed a contract between the original parties;

- they touch and concern the land;

- the burdened party has notice of the covenant, either actual notice or constructive notice, through recording;

- privity exists between the party initially imposing the restriction and the party enforcing it;

- privity exists between the party initially burdened by the restriction and the party against whom it is being enforced.

The person who imposes a covenant running with the land cannot enforce that covenant against a subsequent purchaser of the burdened land unless at that time they are the owner of the land which was intended to be benefited by the covenant.

Zoning ordinances do not automatically override a private restrictive covenant.

Whichever is stricter (i.e., zoning ordinance or covenant) will prevail.

To be binding, a restrictive covenant must be placed on the property at the time when it is conveyed.

The burden cannot be attached to a parcel of land later by someone who has no interest in that parcel of land.

Although the Statute of Frauds applies to covenants, the recording of a deed containing a covenant running with the land by a grantee of land burdened by the covenant is a satisfactory substitute for a memorandum signed by the grantee.

Covenants running with the land can be enforced with injunctive relief.

Common schemes

If the grantor consistently imposes similar covenants on a group of lots in a subdivision, they have created a common scheme.

Two effects of the creation of a common scheme that is not true of covenants, in general, are:

1) the owner of lots burdened by the covenant restrictions can sue the owner of any other lot burdened by the covenant to enforce the restrictions.

2) the grantor can be required to impose similar restrictions on the remaining lots in the subdivision, even if they had not promised in writing to do so.

If there is no common scheme, persons owning lots not owned by the person imposing the restriction when it was imposed cannot enforce the restriction.

Mortgages

Once the property owner validly gives a mortgage, it remains a lien on the property until the obligation securing it is paid in full and the mortgage is discharged, or the holder of the mortgage voluntarily gives a discharge before being required to do so.

If the mortgagor agrees not to transfer the property subject to the mortgage without the mortgagee's consent, the transfer without the mortgagee's consent constitutes a breach of the mortgage, permitting the mortgagee to declare the entire amount of the mortgage note immediately or to foreclose.

The following rules apply when a mortgage is foreclosed.

> If a mortgage foreclosure sale brings more than enough to satisfy the outstanding encumbrance, the balance is paid to satisfy the holders of junior encumbrances, and any remaining balance is paid to the mortgagor.

> A judgment lien is a junior lien to existing mortgages on property held by the debtor when the mortgage lien is filed.

> If the mortgage foreclosure sale brings less than the amount necessary to satisfy the mortgage note and foreclosure expenses, the mortgage note holder may collect the remaining balance on the note from the mortgagor or purchasers from the mortgagor, depending upon the terms of the mortgage and the subsequent transfer of the property.

> The title of a mortgage foreclosure purchaser is not subject to encumbrances placed on the land after the mortgage.

> For example, if O gives a mortgage to A and subsequently gives a mortgage to B, P may take the property free of the mortgage to B if they purchase at the foreclosure of the mortgage to A.

> The foreclosure of a prior mortgage does not eliminate a junior encumbrance unless notice of the mortgage foreclosure is given to the junior encumbrance holder.

> The junior encumbrance holder may still redeem the property from the foreclosing prior mortgagee or still foreclose the mortgage.

> A mortgagee has the right to take possession of the property to preserve it if the mortgagor is in default by failing to make the required payments or breaching other mortgage covenants.

> When a mortgagee takes possession, they assume the tort liabilities of the equitable owner.

When a second mortgage is foreclosed, the purchaser at the foreclosure sale must continue to pay the first mortgage, which remains a valid prior encumbrance on the property.

If the mortgagor has given the mortgagee a mortgage on several parcels of land and has, after that, transferred some of the parcels without discharge of the mortgage, and the mortgage is in default, the mortgagee must first foreclose on the remaining parcel owned by the mortgagor.

Furthermore, if they are not satisfied in full by that foreclosure, they may foreclose on the remaining parcels in the inverse order in which the mortgagor alienated them.

The following rules apply when the property owner who has given a mortgage transfers property without discharging the mortgage.

It the buyer agrees to assume and pay the mortgage, the buyer is primarily liable on the mortgage, and the original mortgagor is only secondarily liable on the mortgage.

If the mortgagor is required to pay the mortgage note, they may collect the amount paid from the buyer who purchased the property.

If the buyer takes subject to the mortgage (i.e., without agreeing to pay the debt), the buyer is not liable for a deficiency judgment on the mortgage note in the event of foreclosure but can lose the property through foreclosure if they do not pay the mortgage.

The original mortgagor is still primarily liable for any deficiency judgment on the mortgage notes.

If the mortgagor, buyer, and mortgagee enter into a novation at the time of transfer of the property, the buyer is liable to the mortgagee on the mortgage note, and the mortgagor has no liability on the mortgage note.

The following priorities apply when there are multiple security interests on the property.

A mortgage given by the purchaser to the former owner as a part of the property's purchase price, which is recorded immediately after the deed, takes precedence over other liens placed on the property at the time of the conveyance.

The holder of a valid personal property security interest has the right to remove that property on default over a mortgagee's objections who held a valid lien on the real estate when the personal property was affixed to the land.

The following rules apply to equitable mortgages, which occur when the property owner gives a deed rather than a mortgage to secure a debt, with the understanding that the creditor will deed the property back to the debtor when the debt is paid.

> Neither the *parol evidence rule* nor the *Statute of Frauds* prevents the debtor from proving by oral evidence that a mortgage transaction rather than a sale was intended when the debtor gave a deed to the creditor.

> When the debt has been repaid, the debtor can require a reconveyance of the property if the title is held by the creditor or someone knowing the deed constituted an equitable mortgage.

> If the creditor has transferred title to a *bona fide* purchaser, the debtor cannot obtain the property's reconveyance but can obtain damages from the creditor.

> If the debtor defaults on the payment of the debt secured by an equitable mortgage, the creditor is not the property's automatic owner but must foreclose the mortgage under state law.

The mortgagor of a property may do such acts on the mortgaged property, including removing part of the building, which is part of the mortgaged premises during good husbandry.

When there is an outstanding mortgage on real estate when the testator dies and devises it, the devisees take the property subject to the mortgage unless the testator requires the executor to discharge the mortgage with other assets of the estate.

Other security devices

Other security devices (e.g., installment sales contracts), where the purchaser is given possession of the property but does not receive a deed until all installments are paid, are treated as a mortgage by a court.

Appropriate procedures required for foreclosure and redemption to protect the owner's equity are required if the property's possessor defaults on their obligation.

Choice of property devices

Covenants that run with the land are the most useful property devices to control land use without harming the title's marketability.

Covenants require that the person enforcing them must own the benefited land.

Easements are useful when limited use of a parcel is desired for an indefinite period.

A conditional fee simple, which takes the title away from the party in possession if they breach their obligations, is useful only where the marketability of the possessor's property interest is not an issue.

The holder of the residuary interest who will take if the condition is broken need not be the owner of any benefited land.

Zoning and other forms of governmental control are limited because they are subject to change by the political process.

Water rights

Under the common law, each landowner through whose land a watercourse flows have the right to make reasonable use of the water.

In determining reasonable use, domestic uses such as drinking water and water for toilets and washing are superior to artificial uses such as irrigation.

In states where riparian rights are governed by the doctrine of *prior appropriation*, the first riparian user to appropriate water for use has the right to continue to use that quantity of water even to the detriment of other riparian owners.

Water from melting snows and rain is diffuse surface water. A landowner may impound diffuse surface waters if they do not do so maliciously.

Notes for active learning

Vendor and Purchaser

Statute of Frauds

An action for specific performance of a land contract must ordinarily satisfy the Statute of Frauds.

The Statute of Frauds is satisfied if a memorandum signed by the party to be charged contains the essential terms of the agreement, namely, the price and an adequate description of the property.

The requirement of a memorandum signed by the party to be charged is not applicable if there are actions that constitute a part performance.

A deposit is not necessary to make a written purchase and sale agreement enforceable, which satisfies the Statute of Frauds.

The Statute of Frauds applies to an agreement among co-owners to change how they hold the property (e.g., change from a tenancy in common to joint tenancy).

An oral agreement to waive the application of the Statute of Frauds is not effective.

The Statute of Frauds is not satisfied by a memorandum creating a brokerage contract.

Payment of the purchase price by the buyer and acceptance by the seller is not sufficient part performance to take an oral agreement out of the Statute of Frauds.

Part performance

If there is no written agreement, a court of equity can specifically enforce an oral agreement to convey if the part performance doctrine is satisfied.

In all cases, there must be an oral agreement to purchase the land relied upon by the purchaser to their detriment.

Part performance is satisfied in many jurisdictions if the seller engaged in equitable fraud.

In other jurisdictions, the court will order a conveyance only if the conduct of the parties unequivocally proves that an oral agreement to convey existed.

This test is ordinarily satisfied when the purchaser pays the purchase price, has possession of the land with the seller's permission, and improves the land.

This test is known as the *unequivocal referability* theory.

Enforceability of purchase and sale agreements by specific performance

Buyers and sellers have the right to specifically enforce purchase and sale agreements for land as well as the right to a damage remedy.

Rights under a purchase and sale agreement survive the deaths of the seller or buyer and may be enforced by the executors of their respective estates.

Equitable conversion

Because buyer and seller have the right to specific performance of a contract to sell land, the doctrine of equitable conversion fixes the time of the property transformation from personalty to realty when a binding purchase and sale agreement is executed by buyer and seller.

Where the doctrine is applicable, upon the execution of a binding purchase and sale agreement, the buyer's interest is immediate in realty, and the seller's interest is immediate in personalty.

The risk of loss is on the buyer when a binding purchase and sale agreement is executed.

A binding purchase and sale agreement recorded serves as notice to any subsequent purchaser from the seller, preventing them from becoming a *bona fide* purchaser.

Time of closing

If a purchase and sale agreement contains a provision that "time is of the essence," the seller and the buyer are in default if they do not close or tender performance on the date specified in the agreement.

If a purchase and sale agreement does not contain a provision that "time is of the essence," each party must close within a reasonable time, and neither is in default if they fail to close on the date specified in the agreement.

Marketable title

A seller need not own the property or have marketable title to it when entering into a purchase and sale agreement for the agreement to be valid.

If a purchase and sale agreement is silent concerning the title to be conveyed, the seller is required to deliver a marketable title.

The title of the holder of a fee simple determinable or a fee simple subject to a condition subsequent is not marketable.

The title is not marketable if an undivided interest is not being conveyed or an encumbrance is not to be discharged.

The limitation placed by a zoning ordinance on the property's future use does not render the title unmarketable.

If the property violates a zoning ordinance at the time set for closing, the title is unmarketable.

If the title would expose a potential buyer to litigation, which is not frivolous, the seller's title is unmarketable.

A person who has obtained title to the property by adverse possession does not have marketable title unless the title has been confirmed in a judicial proceeding.

A seller's obligation to deliver marketable title occurs at the time of the closing. The seller can use portions of the purchase price to pay off encumbrances, which would otherwise destroy marketable title.

Survival of covenants in the purchase and sale agreement

If the buyer accepts a deed to fulfill the seller's obligations under a purchase and sale agreement, the covenants in the purchase and sale agreement are no longer enforceable unless the agreement states that they survive the closing.

Nevertheless, the buyer has the right to sue for a breach of warranty of the deed's covenants.

Failure to disclose hidden defects

Failure by the seller to disclose a latent material defect that could not be discovered by inspection will give the buyer a right to sue for damages or rescind the transaction.

Notes for active learning

Title

Delivery and validity of a deed

To be valid, the grantor must sign a deed, adequately describe the property to be conveyed, and adequately describe the grantee.

Consideration is not needed for a deed to be valid.

Consideration is necessary to enforce a promise to convey property.

A fraudulently altered release, a forged deed, or an undelivered deed stolen is null and conveys no title.

Even if the instrument is recorded, a *bona fide* purchaser who relies on it in good faith is not protected.

If a deed is placed into escrow as part of a commercial real estate transaction and the transaction is completed, the transfer of title is when the deed was delivered into escrow.

The recording does not deprive a grantor of a cause of action to rescind a conveyance against their immediate grantee.

The recording system protects only an innocent purchaser from the immediate grantee.

Title to real estate is transferred from the grantor to the grantee when the grantor delivers a validly executed deed to the grantee, even if the deed is not recorded.

Handing the deed to the grantee or their agent raises a rebuttable presumption of delivery.

The fact that a deed has been recorded raises a presumption that it has been delivered.

The original deed's subsequent redelivery, which has not been recorded from the grantee to the grantor, does not retransfer title to the grantor.

A new deed signed by the grantee to the grantor is required to revest title in the grantor.

A valid transfer of title requires the delivery of a valid deed, which the grantee has accepted.

Acceptance is presumed if the gift is beneficial.

The title has not been transferred if the grantee has affirmatively indicated that they have not accepted the deed.

The existence of a grantee who is identifiable with certainty is a requirement of a valid deed.

A deed delivered with the grantee intentionally left blank is valid and authorizes the person receiving the deed to fill in the grantee's name.

A deed to a grantee who is dead at the time of conveyance does not convey title to the grantee or their estate.

Unless a deed specifies a lesser interest (e.g., a life estate), a deed conveys a fee simple interest.

A gift *causa mortis* may only be made of personal property.

A gift may be made of real estate.

A deed is required as an element for a gift.

Description of property

The property must be described with reasonable certainty to satisfy the condition that the property conveyed be reasonably identified in a deed.

A reference in a deed to a survey or plan is sufficient to identify the property, even if the survey or plan is not recorded.

If the deed description can not determine the exact location of the property conveyed, *parol evidence* is admissible to clarify the parties' intent.

If it is not possible to describe the property conveyed from the contents of the deed itself or with the aid of ancillary procedures, the deed is invalid.

For a *metes and bounds* description of the property, a conflict between distances set forth in the deed and monuments on the ground, the monuments prevail over distance.

If a property boundary describes a private way, the owner owns to the midpoint of the way.

If the deed to property understates the acreage that the parties intended to convey, the grantee is entitled to have an equity court reform the deed to reflect the correct acreage conveyed.

If abutters, uncertain of their exact boundary, fix a line by agreement, either oral or written, and abide by the boundary line, the agreement is valid and enforceable in fixing the boundary even though the boundary is fixed by their respective deeds may be different.

Covenants of title

A quitclaim deed contains no covenants so that the grantee has no claim under the deed against the grantor if the title is defective.

A warranty deed contains present covenants, such as a covenant with no encumbrances on the property, which run only to the grantee and not to their successors.

Present covenants are breached, if at all, at the time of conveyance and thus are limited by a statute of limitations which starts at the time of the conveyance.

A warranty deed contains future covenants that run to the grantee and successors.

The future covenant of quiet enjoyment is breached when the grantee or successor in title is ousted from possession from all or part of the land by one having a superior title.

The covenants of title in a warranty deed do not carry the obligation to pay for a title defense.

There is no requirement that a grantee who receives a deed with covenants need be a *bona fide* purchaser to sue the grantor for breach of warranty if the covenants are not true.

Estoppel by deed

Estoppel by deed applies to validate a deed (e.g., warranty deed) executed and delivered by a grantor who had no title to the land at that time but who represented that they have such title and who after that acquired such title.

For example, A gives a warranty deed of Blackacre to B when A does not own it, and A later acquires title from O, the true owner. B is the property owner without the delivery of a new deed when A acquires title from O.

Operation of the recording system

A deed or other instrument delivered need not be recorded to be effective for the original parties to the transaction.

A *bona fide* purchaser (BFP) who is a subsequent grantee prevails over a prior grantee who fails to record their deed.

A *bona fide* purchaser takes free of encumbrances on the property given by the grantor, which has not been recorded.

A mortgage lien does not automatically have priority over a judgment lien.

A mortgagee who loans money after a judgment lien is recorded is considered to have constructive notice of the judgment lien and cannot be a *bona fide* purchaser and does not have priority over judgment liens.

If O, the owner of the property, delivers a deed to a grantee A and A records immediately, but O then subsequently delivers a deed of the same property to another grantee B, B loses in an action against A because they cannot be a *bona fide* purchaser with respect to a deed that has been properly recorded.

The issue of if grantee prevails does not turn on whether the first grantee is a *bona fide* purchaser.

The inquiry of a *bona fide* purchaser is relevant only for the second grantee.

If A receives and promptly records a deed to the property as a gift and is thus not a purchaser, A prevails in an action by B, a subsequent grantee, even if B paid O for an interest in the property.

The act of recording a valid purchase and sale agreement establishes the purchaser's order of priority in determining rights against subsequent grantees or subsequent lien holders.

The recording system does not protect *bona fide* purchasers who acquire from a person who appears to have good record title but who obtained title by a forged deed.

Bona fide purchasers who acquire from a person who has good record title but who has lost the title by adverse possession are not protected by the recording system and will lose to the person acquiring title by adverse possession.

For example:

The following scenario demonstrates a deed recorded out of order in the chain of title in the recording system:

1) A deeds to B with a warranty deed, but A does not own the property.

2) B records.

3) O, the true owner, deeds to A.

Under the doctrine of estoppel by deed, the deed passes immediately to B.

The deed from A to B is valid even though it is recorded before A had title.

In this case, someone searching the title would not find the deed from A to B, which made B the property owner if they were searching O's name in the grantor index. A search would find the deed from O to A.

The same problem occurs, in the following scenario, when the grantee records late:

1) O deeds to A.

2) A fails to record promptly.

3) O deeds to B as a gift. B records.

4) A records.

In this case, B prevails as the owner over A. Someone searching title would not find the deed from O to A in the grantor index if they searched A's name until O alienated the property by deeding to B.

In each case, a subsequent purchaser can be a *bona fide* purchaser and prevail over the true owner because the deed recorded out of order is not constructive notice to a subsequent *bona fide* purchaser.

If a subsequent *bona fide* purchaser obtains title, the prior grantee has no further interest in the property.

For example, if O deeds to A who does not record and then deeds to B, a subsequent *bona fide* purchaser, and B then deeds to C, who knows of the deed from O to A, C will prevail over A because B prevails over A.

Characteristics of a *bona fide* purchaser

Not all persons who might have an interest in property are "purchasers" who have the protection of the recording system.

Judgment lien holders are frequently denied protection.

A statute frequently used in multistate questions provides:

> *"Any judgment properly filed shall, for ten years from filing, be a lien on the real property then owned or subsequently acquired by any person against whom the judgment is rendered."*

If such a statute is in effect, the judgment lien, even though recorded, does not prevail against an owner who took from the person against whom the judgment was rendered but did not record their deed before the judgment was recorded.

A person who takes a conveyance in satisfaction of a prior debt is considered a purchaser in most jurisdictions.

A person need not search title and rely on the registry records to qualify as a *bona fide* purchaser, although they would be charged with the notice that such a search would provide.

If the subsequent grantee has actual knowledge of the deed to the prior grantee, they cannot prevail even if the prior grantee's deed is not properly recorded.

Facts that would be discovered by an inspection of the property and lead to a further inquiry can destroy a buyer's status as a *bona fide* purchaser.

Even though a donee is not a purchaser and will not prevail over a prior grantee who has not recorded, a *bona fide* purchaser from the donee prevails over a prior grantee if the prior grantee has not properly recorded at the time that the purchaser from the donee accepts the deed and records.

Types of recording systems

There are two principal types of recording systems:

1) The standard notice type recording statute provides:

"No conveyance or mortgage of real property shall be good against subsequent purchasers for value and without notice unless the same be recorded according to law."

2) The standard race-notice recording system provides:

"No unrecorded conveyance or mortgage of real property shall be good against subsequent purchasers for value without notice, who shall first record."

The following transactions illustrate the difference between the standard notice and standard race-notice systems:

1) O, the owner of Blackacre conveys to A.

2) O, then conveys to B a purchaser for value who has no notice of the deed to A.

3) A records.

4) B records.

B prevails in a notice jurisdiction because A had not recorded at the time B paid consideration and received a deed.

In a race-notice jurisdiction, A prevails even though B is a *bona fide* purchaser because A recorded before B.

Landlord–tenant relationship

A landlord-tenant relationship arises when the owner, or possessor of property, grants a party the exclusive use of the property for some time.

A lessor who knows of a hidden defect in the premises must warn the tenant about that defect.

If a landlord denies a tenant the beneficial use of the property and the tenant moves out, the former tenant is not liable to pay rent because the denial of that beneficial use is a constructive eviction.

Under the doctrine of retaliatory eviction, a landlord cannot lawfully terminate a month-to-month tenancy or bring eviction proceedings at the termination of a lease if this action is a retaliation for the tenant's exercise of their legal rights (e.g., reporting building code violations).

The landlord, not the tenant, is the beneficiary of a covenant not to assign a lease and has a right to waive the covenant.

Types of tenancies

A periodic tenancy arises when there is no written lease, and the tenant occupies the property and pays rent periodically.

A periodic tenancy occurs when the tenant continues to occupy at the end of the lease term.

The duration of a periodic tenancy is determined by the length of the period between rent payments.

A periodic tenancy is terminated by notice from one party to the other, given before the commencement of a rental period.

A term for years is a tenancy of a fixed duration. Except for short-term leases of less than one year, the Statute of Frauds applies to a term for years.

A term for years is terminated at the end of the term without notice by either party.

If the tenant holds over, a periodic tenancy is created when the landlord accepts rent after the lease term.

A tenant at sufferance occurs when a tenant has entered the property under either a term for years or a periodic tenancy, and that tenancy has been terminated.

A landlord may bring immediate eviction proceedings against a tenant at sufferance.

Assignment and subletting of tenancies

The tenant must pay rent during the entire term because of the lease contract unless the landlord, tenant, and assignee enter into a novation, in which case the assignee has the contractual obligation to pay rent, and the tenant is no longer liable for the rent.

If the lease is silent, the tenant may assign their lease and sublet the property.

A covenant against assignment does not prevent a tenant from subletting the property.

An assignee is a person who has received from a tenant an assignment of their entire remaining leasehold interest.

A person can become an assignee and entitled to possession even if they have not contractually assumed the obligations of the lease.

Even if not contractually obligated on the lease, an assignee is obligated to pay rent to the landlord during the leasehold property's possession because they are in privity of estate with the landlord.

If an assignee is no longer privity to an estate because they further assigned the lease, they are not obligated to pay rent unless they have contractually assumed the lease obligations.

When a tenant validly assigns a lease, and the assignee assumes the lease, the assignee, and the landlord (or the landlord's successors) are bound by the covenants in the lease running with the land.

Examples include a covenant to pay taxes or a covenant granting the tenant a right to purchase the property.

If the tenant enters into a subtenancy, leasing the property for a term less than the remaining term, there is a new leasehold between the tenant, who is in effect a landlord, and the subtenant.

Where a subtenancy is created, there is no privity of estate between the subtenant and the landlord, and the subtenant is not obligated to pay rent to the landlord unless they agree explicitly.

Licenses

A *license* is permission to use the land of another.

It may be oral, written, or implied.

A license is revocable and is not subject to the Statute of Frauds.

Licenses are created when the occupier of land does not have an exclusive right of possession.

In contrast to a lease, a license permits the holder of a license to occupy the property but creates no property interest in the occupier.

If they hold the license according to a contract, they cannot specifically enforce the contract.

For a license to be irrevocable because of estoppel, the holder of the license must have justifiably incurred a detriment, such as the expenditure of funds to upgrade the property subject to a license in reliance upon an agreement not to revoke it.

Easements, Profits and Licenses

Easement, profits, and licenses are rights to *use* land compared to an estate, a right to *possess* land.

Use rights may be called *servitudes*.

A *covenant* (i.e., an agreement) is a servitude.

A *servitude* is the rights or obligations of ownership or possession running with the land.

Easements and *profits* are property interests that can be granted expressly.

Such grant should be in writing to satisfy the statute of frauds as applied to the transfer of real property interests.

Easements and profits generally have a fixed term or a defeasible term like other property interests.

A *license* is a use right not subject to the statute of frauds as a personal property interest.

The duration of ownership rights defines easement.

An easement is assumed to last forever unless the conveyance indicates a contrary intent; analogous to transfers of an estate typically assumed to transfer a *fee simple absolute* unless the conveyance indicates a contrary intent.

An easement can:

> last forever, analogous to a *fee simple absolute* interest in an estate.
>
> be made conditional, analogous to a *defeasible estate*.
>
> be created to last for a fixed period, analogous to a *lease* of an estate.
>
> be created to last for a person's lifetime, analogous to a *life estate*.

Types and categories of use rights

An *easement* is a right to use the land of another.

A *profit* permits removing items from another's land (e.g., minerals, sand, timber).

A *license* is an easement revocable at will by the licensor (i.e., the grantor of the right).

> 1) Normally, a license is not assignable or inheritable as a personal right of the licensee.
>
> 2) A license can be expressly created.

3) An easement or profit that fails to comply with a necessary legal requirement (e.g., the statute of frauds) becomes a license by default.

4) A license is an *easement at will*.

In gross *vs.* appurtenant easements and profits

An *easement in gross* is a right allowing the use of another's property.

An easement in gross benefits the property owner and not the property.

An easement in gross cannot be transferred.

An *appurtenant easement* applies to the property, even if the owners change.

1) The use right and the land cannot be owned separately. The use right *runs with the land* (i.e., conveyed with the land), so the landowner owns the use right.

2) *Dominant estate* has the benefit of the use right.

3) *Servient estate* has the burdened by the use right.

If there is no dominant estate (only servient estate) typically, it would be an *in gross* use right.

As a matter of judicial construction, courts prefer appurtenant easements over in gross easements.

If it is unclear if an easement is in gross or appurtenant, the court tends to find an appurtenant easement.

To determine if a use right is appurtenant or in gross, the court examines if the purpose of use right is for the benefit of the landowner separate from the land.

Affirmative and negative easements

Affirmative easements allow the easement owner to act on the servient estate; not be allowed but for the easement.

For example, Able owns an easement to walk across Baker's land to reach the public highway. This is affirmative easement because it allows Able to cross Baker's land, which would be an act of trespass, but for the easement.

Negative easements allow the easement owner to prevent the servient estate from doing an act on the servient estate, which the servient estate would be allowed but for the easement.

Many courts have been reluctant to expand the use of negative easements.

For example, Able owns property that is separated from the ocean by Baker's property. Able has an easement over Baker's adjacent property, entitling Able to an unobstructed view of the ocean, which is a negative easement.

Transfer of easements and profits

The intent of parties at the creation of easement or profit determines if it is transferable.

Absent contrary intent, the following rules are presumed:

1) Appurtenant easements and profits transfer with the land without regard to mention in the transfer.

2) In gross easements and profits:

   If *non-commercial*, they are not usually freely transferable,

   If *commercial*, they are generally transferable.

Commercial means the use right was created primarily for economic benefit.

Apportionability and divisibility of easements and profits

The intent of the parties creating the use right controls.

Appurtenant easement and profit – absent contrary intent, these rules are presumed:

1) Division of the appurtenant easement or profit occurs by dividing the property affected by the easement. Appurtenant easements are divisible (or apportionable) absent the contrary intent of the parties.

2) Division of the servient estate:

   A. If a servient estate is divided, each remains subject to the burden of the estate or profit.

An exception to the burden of the servient estate is when, before the division of the servient estate, the burden was located on a specific portion of the servient estate, only the servient estate where the burden was located is still subject to the burden.

For example, a servient estate is subject to the burden of pipeline easement. The land is divided with the pipeline left on one portion. Only a portion of the divided property with the pipeline has the burden of the easement.

Division of the dominant estate

Division of the dominant estate results in each portion of the dominant estate usually granted the proportionate benefit of the easement or profit.

In gross easement or profit – absent contrary intent these rules are presumed:

1) Exclusive easements and profits are freely divisible (or apportionable).

2) Non-exclusive easement or profits not divisible.

If there is an increased burden on land due to division/apportioning of easement or profit:

    1)   Rights of easement owner and rights of servient estate owner must be balanced:

          A. Servient owner's use must not unduly interfere with use by the easement owner,

          B. Division of the easement must not unduly burden the servient estate.

    2) Consideration is whether division results in an increased burden on the servient estate. If an increased burden results from division, then less likely division will be allowed. However, if there is no increased burden from the division, it is more likely that division will be allowed.

Creation of easements and profits

Easements and profits can be created by express grant; this must be in writing to satisfy the statute of frauds.

Easements and profits can be created by actions involving effort or money based on reliance on a license.

    1)   This is of reliance is based on *estoppel* theory,

    2)   Such a servitude is an *irrevocable license.*

Easements can be created by implication (i.e., implied easements).

Implied easements are based on the legal fiction (theory) that even though parties did not expressly create an easement, it is presumed they must have intended to create an easement considering the facts.

    1)   *Implied reservation* – grantor conveys a servient estate and retains the dominant estate; the grantor is held to have impliedly reserved an easement in the servient estate.

    2)   *Implied grant* – grantor conveys a dominant estate; the grantor is held to have impliedly granted the owner of the dominant estate an easement in the servient estate.

Implied easements based on *prior use*

Implied easements based on *prior use* of the commonly owned property before severance requires:

1) common ownership of the property before the severance;

2) severance of the property into separate parcels owned by different parties;

3) before severance, part of the land was apparently, continuously, and permanently used for the benefit of another part of the land (i.e., *quasi-easement*); and

4) continuation of the use right after severance is necessary for the use of the dominant estate.

Implied easement *based on necessity*

Implied easement *based on necessity* requires:

1) severance of property into parcels owned by different parties; and

2) severance creates the necessity for an easement.

Implied easements by necessity typically end when the necessity for the easement terminates.

The triggering of termination above is not valid for implied easements based on prior use.

Easements created by prescription

Early prescriptive easement theory was premised on the *lost grant theory.*

If the easement existed for an extended period, it is presumed that the easement was a grant, but due to the passage of time, evidence of the grant has been lost.

The *lost grant theory* is not prevalent, but references are seen in cases.

Under the modern theory, an easement by prescription amounts to adverse possession of an easement; and courts apply the requirements of adverse possession to deem prescriptive easements.

Requirements of *easement by prescription*, the use of another's property must be:

Actual

Open and notorious

Hostile

Continuous

A difference between adverse possession (i.e., acquiring an estate) and prescriptive easements (i.e., right of use) is that adverse possession has a requirement of *exclusive possession.*

No exclusive use requirement exists for an easement by prescription.

Scope of easements

Express easements:

1)   Interpret language conveying the easement.

2)   Intent of the parties creating the easement controls.

If the scope of the easement is ambiguous or limitless, general rules apply:

> A court presumes reasonable use of the easement, balancing the interests of the dominant and servient estate holders so that the dominant owner can use the easement for reasonable use of the dominant estate, and the servient owner will not be unreasonably burdened by the dominant owner's use of the easement.

> Courts presume that parties intend to change the scope of the easement with technology, consistent with changes in the surrounding area and normal development of the dominant estate.

> Appurtenant easements can only be exercised for the benefit of the dominant estate.

> Dominant estates cannot be enlarged without the consent of all parties.

Implied easements

Construe the scope of the easement consistent with circumstances leading to the creation of the implied easement.

Construe the scope of the easement consistent with circumstances leading to the creation of the expressed easement.

Prescriptive easements

The scope of an easement by prescription is fixed by the use through which it was created (i.e., use during the prescription period).

The use of an easement made during the prescription period does not fix the scope of the easement.

The scope of the easement can change to satisfy evolving needs, but such changes can not be substantial.

The change in scope must be consistent with the general pattern formed by the original adverse use.

Repair and maintenance of an easement

Absent a contrary agreement, the easement owner must maintain and repair the easement.

Use of easement by servient estate owner and third parties

Language in the grant of the easement controls uses by the servient estate owner and third parties.

If the easement is exclusive, the servient owner and third parties have no right to use the easement.

If an easement is not an exclusive easement, the servient owner retains the right to use the easement, provided such use does not interfere unreasonably with use by the easement owner.

If the servient owner has the right to use an easement, they can convey or grant to others who can use the easement provided that such use does not interfere unreasonably with the use of the easement by the easement owner.

In determining whether use by servient owner or third party is reasonable, courts use a *rule of reason* approach to balance the parties' interests in the absence of controlling language in the grant of the easement.

The use of an easement by third parties is subordinate to the use by the easement owner.

Termination of an easement

Easements terminate by the terms of the easement.

For example:

>Easement for ten years ends after ten years.

>Easement for someone's life ends at their death.

>Easement with defeasible terms(i.e., based on a condition subsequent) ends upon the condition.

Easements terminate by express agreement; the easement and servient estate owners can agree to end the easement.

This agreed termination must be accomplished via a written conveyance; the *release* is a writing required by the Statute of Frauds for an interest in land.

Extinguishment results from the following:

> 1) Abandonment   non use of easement by the easement owner coupled with an intent to abandon. Intent can be shown (implied) by the actions of the parties and circumstances.

> 2) Prescription – servient owner uses the easement in a manner inconsistent with the easement, and the requirements of easement by prescription are met. The servient owner can extinguish the easement once the statutory period is satisfied.

> 3) Estoppel – easement can be extinguished by estoppel. The easement owner can be estopped from asserting easement when the servient owner, in reasonable reliance on the conduct of the easement owner, has used land inconsistent with the easement, and it inequitable to permit further use of the easement.

An example of estoppel, the servient owner builds a house across the easement (i.e., right of way), and the dominant owner does not object even though aware that the house is being built on their right of way.

Leases

Leaseholds are real property interests.

A lease provides the leaseholder with the right of possession – some courts use a *control test* for possession.

Under the *control test*, the question is how much control the person had over the property.

1)   Total control amounts to possession.

2)   No control does not constitute possession.

If a person has the right to use the land with no right to possession, they have a mere *use* right.

If grantor retains possession of land but grants someone the right to remove something from the land (e.g., soil) that is a profit (mere grant of privilege to remove something from land) as distinguished from granting the right of possession of the land.

Landlord (modern term is *lessor*) is the property owner who transfers, conveys, or grants the leasehold to another according to a lease.

According to a lease, the *tenant* (or *lessee*) is the *transferee* (*conveyee* or *grantee*) for a leasehold property.

Leasehold types

Term for years (or *estate for years*) – lease for a fixed or set term.

Terminates automatically at the end of lease term.

Generally created by agreement of the parties.

Periodic tenancy – lease that extends for successive periods.

Essentially of *indefinite duration*.

A lease can be established by *express agreement* or by the action of the parties (i.e., *impliedly*).

A lease can be established by a court finding an express lease to be legally defective due to the statute of frauds. If established this way, the period of lease created generally found to be the period for which rent is stated in the defective agreement or, if no agreement, generally for a period for which rent is paid regularly.

The term is six months for year-to-year periodic tenancy at common law.

Statutes in most states set a notice period.

Termination is by either party upon proper notice.

Tenancy at will – lessees must have possession by permission.

No agreed lease term.

Terminates at the will of either lessor or lessee without any notice requirement.

Tenancy at sufferance (or *holdover tenancy*) – lessee in rightful possession holds over at the end of the lease term.

Lessor can treat tenant at sufferance as a trespasser and sue for damages – fair rental (and ejectment).

Lessor can elect to treat lessee as tenant and demand rental.

Landlord's duty with respect to title and possession burdened by implied covenants.

Covenants

Covenant of power to demise: lessor covenants the power to convey leasehold by lease.

Covenant of quiet enjoyment:

1) Lessor covenants lessee will have the legal right to possession of leasehold at the beginning of lease;

2) Right of possession will not be wrongfully disturbed by the lessor; and

3) Right of possession will not be disturbed by 3rd parties who have a right to possession superior to lessee's right of possession

A covenant that the lessor provides the lessee actual leasehold possession at the beginning of the lease term.

A covenant that the lessor provides the lessee actual leasehold possession depends on jurisdiction:

English rule: implied covenant that lessee can get possession at the beginning of the lease term.

American rule: no implied covenant that lessee can get possession at the start of a lease – up to lessee to bring an action to remove a holdover tenant – not lessor's responsibility.

Duties for fitness and repair of the leased property

Common law rule concerning the fitness of leased property is caveat emptor. The lessee rents property at their peril and takes the risk of fitness of the property.

Common law rule is that the obligation of the lessee to pay rent continues even if the property is unfit for any use.

Common law rule concerning repair and upkeep of the leased property is that these obligations shift to the lessee.

Common law rule – if an act of God destroys a property that is part of leasehold, the lessee is not obligated to replace the destroyed property; but the lessee liable to pay rent.

Compare the above rules with common law waste law.

The above common law obligations can be shifted by agreement of the parties.

Also, the shift by courts from viewing leases as pure real property conveyances to applying contract theory enables courts to rely on various contract doctrines to end leases, such as *commercial frustration* or *impossibility of performance* in appropriate cases.

Illegality terminates leases

If the lease limits the use of the property to some legal and some illegal uses, the lease is enforceable.

If the lease limits the use of the property to only illegal uses lease usually unenforceable

If the lease limits the use of the property to use not permitted by zoning law, the lease enforceable if zoning law has a system for allowing variances (most zoning laws allow for variances).

Abandonment and surrender

Abandonment is a unilateral relinquishment of the leasehold by the lessee (does not end lease).

Surrender is mutual agreement of lessor/lessee to end lease (the effect is to end/terminate lease)

Surrender may be expressed or implied.

When a tenant abandons leasehold, the lessor, at common law, can elect one of the following actions:

> 1) Lessor can terminate the lease and retake possession of the leasehold (this action by lessor ends tenant's obligation to pay rent).

> 2) Lessor can leave premises vacant and sue (at an appropriate time) for the entire rent due under the lease.

> 3) Lessor can notify lessee that she is not accepting lessee's abandonment (therefore no surrender) and that lessor will attempt to re-let the property to mitigate damages (lessee liable for total rent less mitigation by lessor due to re-rental of the property).

Lessor must be careful their attempt to mitigate is not construed to equal implied surrender since surrender would terminate the lessee's liability on the lease after the date of surrender.

Most jurisdictions now require lessor of residential property to mitigate damages when the lessee abandons the property. Essentially, some courts eliminate option two above (i.e., the lessor cannot leave premises vacant and sue for the entire rental due under lease; there is an obligation to mitigate damages).

Actual eviction

Lessor ousts lessee either totally or partially from leasehold.

Lessor must physically interfere with the lessee's possession.

The effect of actual eviction is to end the lessee's obligation to pay rent (lease terminates).

The law recognizes partial evictions.

Constructive eviction

Lessor interferes substantially with the lessee's use/enjoyment of property.

Act of lessor must be wrongful (i.e., violation of a duty owed to the tenant).

Lessee must vacate leasehold property to claim constructive eviction.

The effect of constructive eviction is to end the lessee's obligation to pay rent (lease terminates).

Warranty of habitability

The implied *warranty of habitability* of the lease requires the lessor to maintain the property in a safe and habitable condition. The obligation cannot be disclaimed.

Warranty of habitability is restricted to residential leases generally.

The warranty of habitability changed the common law rules, and the lessee caveat was eliminated.

The obligation to pay rent conditioned on lessor not breaching warranty of habitability.

The lessor is now responsible for repairs, unlike contrary rules under common law.

Remedies for breach of habitability

Recission of a lease involves canceling a contract and treating it as though it never existed by ensuring that all its effects are eliminated. Parties are returned to their original state; things exchanged, such as money, must be returned.

Reformation of a lease is a **civil claim brought in by a lawsuit**. With reformation, a judge formally orders a correction to the contract. For example, the judge might **add, delete, or re-word the language** of the lease contract.

Contract damages are the difference between fair market rental of property in compliance with the warranty of habitability and the value of the property with defects.

Punitive damages are damages for annoyance and discomfort (tort).

Assignment and subletting

Assignment of leasehold is when the lessee transfers her entire interest in the leasehold to another party (metaphorically, *the assignee steps into the lessee's shoes*).

Sublease of leasehold is when the lessee transfers less than their entire interest in the leasehold to another party.

The sublessee is not bound by an agreement between lessor and lessee generally.

Assignees are bound by an agreement between the lessor and lessee concerning lease terms connected with the property. Generally, the lessee remains contractually liable to the lessor without regard to the assignment or sublease of the lease by the lessee.

The word "assignment," as used for leaseholds, is a *word of art* with a specific meaning. "Assignment" is used in contract law, but it has a different meaning in contract law. When used for leaseholds, assignment means a conveyance of the leasehold from the lessee to the assignee.

Notes for active learning

Foreclosure Process

A person who owns a piece of real property has an ownership interest in that property. This interest is generally described in writing, known as a deed. A property owner who borrows money from a creditor may use this interest as collateral to repay the loan. This type of collateral arrangement, known as a mortgage, is a two-party transaction.

The owner-debtor is the mortgagor, and the creditor is the mortgagee. If a mortgagor defaults on a mortgage, the mortgagee can declare the entire debt due and payable immediately. This right can be enforced through a legal procedure called foreclosure. All states permit foreclosure sales. Under this method, the debtor's default may trigger a legal court action for foreclosure.

Any party having an interest in the property—including owners of the property and other mortgagees or lienholders—must be named a defendant. If the mortgagee's case is successful, the court will issue a judgment that orders the real property to be sold at a judicial sale. The procedures for a foreclosure action and sale are mandated by state statute. Any surplus must be paid to the mortgagor.

Most states permit foreclosure by power of sale, although this must be expressly conferred in the mortgage (or deed of trust). Under a power of sale, the procedure for that sale is contained in the mortgage (or deed of trust), and no court action is necessary.

Some states permit a mortgagee to bring a separate legal action to recover a deficiency from the mortgagor.

Notes for active learning

Establishing Agency

Agency relationships are generally formed by the mutual consent of a principal and an agent, although not always. An agency can arise as an express agency, implied agency, apparent agency, and agency by ratification. The most common form of agency is express agency. In an express agency, the agent has the authority to contract or otherwise act on the principal's behalf as expressly stated in the agency agreement. Additionally, the agent may possess certain implied or apparent authority to act on the principal's behalf.

Express agency occurs when a principal and an agent expressly agree to enter into an agency agreement with each other. Express agency contracts can be oral or written unless the Statute of Frauds stipulates that they must be written. A power of attorney is an example of an express agency. An implied agency is an agency that occurs from the parties' conduct rather than from a prior agreement between them. The facts determine the extent of the agent's authority.

Implied authority can be conferred by *industry custom*, *prior dealing between the parties*, the agent's position, and acts deemed necessary to carry out the agent's duties.

Apparent agency (or *agency by estoppel*) arises when a principal creates the appearance of an agency that does not exist. Where an apparent agency is established, the principal is estopped from denying the agency relationship and is bound to contracts entered into by the apparent agent while acting within the scope of the apparent agency. The principal's actions (not the agent's) create an apparent agency.

An *agency by ratification* occurs when a person misrepresents themself as another's agent when they are not, and the purported principal ratifies (accepts) the unauthorized act. In such cases, the principal is bound to perform, and the agent is relieved of liability for misrepresentation.

Notes for active learning

Conflict of Laws

Law of *situs*

Law of *situs* – the place of the property is to govern as to the capacity of the testator. Also determines marriage, property, mortgages, etc.

For real property, the law of the *situs* determines the disposition and succession of real property. This is necessary to administer and ensure the accuracy of title records.

Only courts of the *situs* can directly affect title to land in that state because states have a strong interest in the property within their borders.

Immovables are of the most considerable concern: exclusive jurisdiction to the state in which they are situated.

Leaseholds are considered immovable.

Pragmatic concerns – recording system for land interests.

Movables – the law of the *situs* does not always apply as there are many exceptions.

Situs is determined at the time of possession.

Location during litigation to avoid forum shopping.

For distribution between spouses, apply the place of marital domicile.

The Restatement for the choice-of-law issues states the rules in which the courts have evolved in accommodation with specific factors.

For property, such rules are sufficiently precise to permit them to be applied in the decision of a case without explicit reference to the factors which underlie them.

Notes for active learning

Real Property – Quick Facts

1. A proposed use (or improvement) of an **express easement** must *not* exceed the scope of the express burden.

2. A **plat** is *only* a representation of a physical survey made of the land. The plat is like a certified copy of an instrument *controlled by the original*. A survey made and marked upon the ground *prevails* if it conflicts with the plat.

3. In a **partial condemnation**, the landlord-tenant relationship continues, as does the tenant's obligation to pay rent for the remaining lease term.

4. **Landlord-tenant** law traditionally refuses to recognize the *frustration of purpose* as grounds for terminating a lease.

5. Where **joint tenant** A informs joint tenant B that they can do something with a portion of the land, and joint tenant B reasonably relies on those statements to their detriment, joint tenant **A is estopped** to its effect.

6. The Statute of Frauds prevents the enforcement of an **oral agreement** concerning an interest in land.

7. **Reasonable Use Doctrine**—concerning underground water use—permits land use that is *not* merely malicious or a waste of water.

8. **Special Exception to Rule Against Perpetuities** for *options to purchase attached to leaseholds*—when the one who holds the option is the current lessee, RAP does *not* apply.

9. If at the time a lease is entered into, the **landlord knows of a dangerous condition** that the tenant could not discover upon reasonable inspection, the landlord has a **duty to disclose** the dangerous condition. The landlord's failure to disclose imputes liability for injury resulting from the condition.

10. When a **tenant continues in possession *after* the termination** of their right to possession, the landlord has *two* choices of action:

    a) treat the holdover as a trespasser and evict under an unlawful detainer statute; or

    b) in their sole discretion, bind the tenant to a new **periodic tenancy**, in which case the **terms and conditions** of the expired tenancy apply to the new tenancy.

11. **Marketable title** is a title **reasonably free from doubt**, which generally means free from encumbrances and good record title.

    Easements are generally considered encumbrances that render title unmarketable. However, courts hold **beneficial easements visible or known** to the buyer are *not* an encumbrance.

12. **Reformation** may be available for a **mutual mistake**.

13. In general, courts presume that **time is *not* of the essence** in land contracts.

14. The **doctrine of equitable conversion** holds that once an enforceable contract of sale for real property is executed, the purchaser's interest is in *real property.* The seller's interest (i.e., right to proceeds) is *personal property.*

Relationship matrix

Notes for active learning

Review Questions

Multiple-choice questions

1. Concurrent ownership of the deceased tenant's interest passes to their estate is a:

A. Joint tenancy

B. Tenancy in common

C. Tenancy by the entirety

D. Community property

2. An estate *pur autre vie* creates a:

A. Temporary interest in personal property

B. Permanent transfer of goods

C. Lifetime interest in real property

D. Transfer of assets upon death

3. Intangible property includes all of the following EXCEPT:

A. Stock certificates

B. Furniture

C. Bonds

D. Copyrights

4. The following type of asset is a commodity:

A. Soybeans

B. Debentures

C. Preferred stock

D. Oil rights

5. Types of future interests include:

    I. Reversion

    II. Remainder

    III. Fee simple

A. I and II only

B. II only

C. II and III only

D. I, II and III

6. Real property includes the following:

    I. Subsurface rights

    II. Stock certificates

    III. Fixtures

A. I only

B. I and II only

C. I and III only

D. III only

7. A landlord-tenant lease of a property for three months is a:

A. Tenancy for years   **C.** Tenancy at will

B. Periodic tenancy   **D.** Tenancy at sufferance

8. The highest form of ownership for real property is a:

A. Fee simple defeasible   **C.** Fee impressive

B. Qualified fee   **D.** Fee simple absolute

9. Adverse possession of property involves:

     I. Possession of the property over a lengthy period

     II. Putting the property owner on notice of the possession

     III. Possessing the property

A. I only   **C.** II and III only

B. I and II only   **D.** I, II and III

10. The Truth-In-Lending Act applies to:

     I. Commercial credit

     II. Consumer credit

     III. Stock trading

A. I only   **C.** II only

B. I and II only   **D.** II and III only

11. In this form of concurrent ownership, there does not exist a right of survivorship:

A. Joint tenancy   **C.** Tenancy in the entirety

B. Tenancy in common   **D.** Community property

12. The Superfund Act concerns:

A. Hazardous wastes   **C.** Climate pollution

B. Air pollution   **D.** Water pollution

13. Under condominium ownership, the owners own an undivided interest in the:

    I. Dwelling unit

    II. Hallways

    III. Recreational facilities

A. I only   **C.** I and III only

B. I and II only   **D.** II and III only

14. Installed kitchen cabinets are:

A. Fixtures   **C.** Chattel

B. Personal property   **D.** Goods

15. The landlord-tenant relationship when a tenant stays beyond their lease term is a:

A. Tenancy for years   **C.** Tenancy at will

B. Periodic tenancy   **D.** Tenancy at sufferance

16. The following are real property transfer documents:

    I. Warranty deed

    II. Quitclaim deed

    III. *res ispa loquitur*

A. I only   **C.** I and II only

B. II only   **D.** I, II and III

17. The document used to convey real property by sale or gift is a:

A. Warranty   **C.** Conveyance

B. Deed   **D.** Title

18. A woman whose engagement has ended takes off her engagement ring and throws it in the office trashcan. The custodian finds it that night while cleaning the office. The ring is:

A. Mislaid   **C.** Abandoned

B. Lost   **D.** Booty

19. Easements are created by:

    I. Implication

    II. Necessity

    III. Prescription

A. I and II only   **C.** III only

B. II only   **D.** I, II and III

True/false questions

20. Land is the most common form of personal property.

    True   False

21. In a community property state, each spouse claims the fruits of their labors.

    True   False

22. Real property can become personal property.

    True   False

23. A cooperative is a form of co-ownership in a multiple-dwelling building in which a corporation owns the building, and the residents own shares in the corporation.

    True   False

24. In a condominium, each unit owner owns only their unit.

    True   False

25. Under common law, innkeepers are held to a strict liability standard for loss to guests' personal property.

    True   False

26. Structures such as cell towers and bridges are not real property.

    True   False

27. In a tenancy in common, the interest of a surviving tenancy passes to the co-tenants.

    True   False

28. A tenant in common may pass along that interest at death.

    True   False

29. A quitclaim deed provides the greatest number of warranties and the most protections.

    True   False

30. A bailment is the transfer of possession, but not title, of personal property.

    True   False

31. Personal property permanently affixed to land or buildings is a fixture.

    True   False

32. The owner of a life estate measured by the tenant's life may pass the life estate by will.

    True   False

33. A freehold estate is when the estate owner has a present possessory interest in the real property.

    True   False

34. A fee simple defeasible grants the owner all the incidents of a fee simple absolute.

    True   False

35. Real estate can be tangible or intangible.

    True   False

36. The Truth-In-Lending Act requires consumers be told whether they can afford the debt.

    True   False

37. Finders of lost property take title to the property.

    True   False

38. Personal property can become real property.

    True   False

Answer keys

1: B	11: B
2: C	12: A
3: B	13: A
4: A	14: A
5: A	15: D
6: C	16: C
7: A	17: B
8: D	18: C
9: D	19: D
10: C	

20: False	31: True
21: False	32: False
22: True	33: True
23: True	34: False
24: False	35: False
25: True	36: False
26: False	37: False
27: False	38: True
28: True	
29: False	
30: True	

Bar Exam Information, Preparation
and
Test-Taking Strategies

STERLING
Test Prep

Introduction to the Uniform Bar Examination (UBE)

Structure of the UBE

The Uniform Bar Examination (UBE) includes 1) the Multistate Bar Examination (MBE), 2) Multistate Essay Examination (MEE), and 3) Multistate Performance Test (MPT).

The MBE has 200 multiple-choice questions accounting for 50% of the UBE.

The MEE has six essays worth 30% of the UBE score.

The MPT has two legal tasks (e.g., complaint, client letter) for 20% of the UBE score.

The Multistate Bar Examination (MBE)

The Multistate Bar Examination consists of 200 four-option multiple-choice questions prepared by the National Conference of Bar Examiners (NCBE).

Of these 200 questions, 175 are scored, and 25 are unscored pretest questions.

Candidates answer 100 questions in the three-hour morning session and the remaining 100 questions in the three-hour afternoon session.

The 175 scored questions are distributed with 25 questions on each of the seven subject areas: Federal Civil Procedure, Constitutional Law, Contracts, Criminal Law and Procedure, Evidence, Real Property, and Torts.

A specified percentage of questions in each subject tests topics in those subjects.

For example, approximately one-third of Evidence questions test hearsay and its exceptions, while approximately one-third of Torts questions test negligence.

Interpreting the UBE score report

Overall score. The National Conference of Bar Examiners (NCBE) states the Uniform Bar Exam (UBE) requires a passing scaled score between 260 to 280. Scores above 280 receive a passing score in every UBE state.

The "percentile" is the number of people that scored lower. If an examinee scored in the 47th percentile, they scored higher than 47% of the examinees (and lower than 53%).

The examinee is first given a "raw score,"; based on the number of correct answers.

The raw score is adjusted by adding points to achieve the "scaled score." The number of points added is determined by a formula that compares the difficulty of the current exam to prior benchmark exams.

The comparative performance of examinees on "control questions" (prior pretest questions) given on previous exams form the basis for determining each exam's difficulty.

MBE scaled score. Examinees receive a scaled score and not an MBE "raw" score (i.e., the number of correct answers). MBE scores are scaled scores calculated by the NCBE through a statistical process used for standardized tests.

According to the NCBE, this statistical process adjusts raw scores on the current exam to account for differences in difficulty compared to previously administered exams. The scaled score is calculated from the raw score, but the NCBE does not publish the conversion formula.

Since the MBE is a scaled score, equating makes it impossible to know precisely how many questions must be answered correctly to receive a particular score. Equating allows scores from different exams to be compared since a specific scaled score represents the same level of knowledge among exams.

The MBE is curved, so just because a score is "close" to passing does not mean you are close. For example, a 124 may be in the 31st percentile and a 136 in the 62nd percentile. A 12-point difference in scaled scores equates to a 31-point percentile difference. If you are in the 120s, much preparation is needed to increase your score.

For most states, aim for a scaled score of 135 to "pass" the MBE. If you are unsure what score you need, divide the passing score by two. For example, if a 270 is needed to pass the bar, divide 268 by two to yield 135 as a threshold score on the MBE.

The importance of the MBE score

A passing MBE score depends on the jurisdiction. In jurisdictions that score on a 200-point scale, the passing score is the overall score. Passing scores are often approximately 135.

For the July 2020 bar exam, the national average MBE score was 146.1, an increase of 5 points from the July 2019 national average of 141.1.

For comparison, on the July 2018 bar, the national average MBE score was 139.5, a decrease of about 2.2 points from the July 2017 national average of 141.7.

How much the MBE contributes depends on the jurisdiction. Each jurisdiction has its policy for the relative weight given to the MBE compared to other bar exam components.

For Uniform Bar Examination (UBE) jurisdictions, the MBE component is 50%.

Most jurisdictions combine the MBE score with the state essay exam score.

The overall state candidates' performance on the MBE controls the raw state essay's conversion to scaled scores. Achieve a scaled MBE score of at least 135 to pass the bar.

MEE and MPT scores

In a UBE score report, there are six scores for the Multistate Essay Exam (MEE) and two for the Multistate Performance Test (MPT). Most states release this information.

Most states grade on a 1–6 scale (some use another scale).

In states grading on a 1–6 scale, 4 is considered a passing score.

The MEE and MPT sections are not weighted equally.

The MEE essays are worth 60%, while the MPT is 40% of the written score.

Many examinees assume that they passed the MPT and MEE portions of the exam. Examine the score report to see how you performed on these portions.

The objective of the Multistate Bar Exam

Working knowledge of the MBE objectives, the skills it tests, how it is drafted, the relationship of the parts of an MBE question, and the testing limitations provide you a substantial advantage in choosing the correct answers to MBE questions and passing the bar.

Knowing which issues are tested and the form in which they are tested makes it more manageable to learn the large body of substantive law.

The MBE's fundamental objective is to measure fairly, and efficiently which law school graduates have the necessary academic qualifications to be admitted to the bar and exceed this threshold.

The multiple-choice exam used to accomplish this objective must be of a consistent level of difficulty.

The level at which the pass decision is made must be achievable by most candidates.

The MBE tests the following skills:

- reading carefully and critically
- identifying the legal issue in a set of facts
- knowing the law that governs the legal issues tested
- distinguish between frequently confused closely-related principles
- making reasonable judgments from ambiguous facts
- understanding how limiting words make plausible-sounding choices wrong
- choosing the correct answer by intelligently eliminating incorrect choices

Notes for active learning

Preparation Strategies for the Bar Exam

An effective bar exam study plan

There are a lot of great ideas about how to prepare. Follow through with these ideas and turn them into persistent action for successful preparation.

A detailed and well-planned study schedule has benefits, such as giving you a sense of control and building confidence and proficiency.

Pick a date about 12-14 weeks before the exam (November for the February exam and April for the July exam) and use it as the start of your active study period.

Start a month earlier than many others to have a month to review as final preparation at the end.

Students have found this effective. Use an elongated prep period as a study schedule.

Most examinees prefer at least two weeks before the exam to review the material.

By planning early, you will have more time. You may want three or four final weeks to review subjects, take timed exams, and ensure that you are prepared to take the exam.

A few notes on schedule management:

> Do not *start* memorizing during your initial review period. You should be learning every week from the beginning of your study schedule. This final prep period is for reviewing and taking timed exams.

> If you stretch the study schedule over several months, plan review weeks into your schedule. For example, every four weeks, use a few days to review the governing law and take timed exams. This is a practical and fruitful approach as you will be more likely to retain the information.

Pick specific dates for specific tasks; this makes it more likely you will complete them.

Make sure the tasks are measurable. (e.g., practice two MEE essays).

Be realistic about the tasks, time, energy, and your ability to complete the items listed as tasks in preparation for the exam.

Remember to take some scheduled breaks from studying.

Exercise, sleep and take care of your physical and mental health.

If you are not in the right mental state preparing for the exam, you will likely be ineffective when studying and are less likely to pass the exam.

Focused studying

Some people are better at multiple choice questions; others do better with essays.

The multiple-choice portion (MBE at 50%) and the essay portion (MEE at 30% and MPT at 20%) are weighted equally.

Doing poorly in one section means it will be challenging to achieve a passing score.

Identify weaknesses early in the preparation process and focus on them.

If you struggle with multiple-choice questions, dedicate extra time to practicing MBE questions.

If you struggle with writing, focus on completing MEE essays and complete MPT practice materials.

By reviewing your performance on released multiple-choice practice tests, be concerned if you consistently miss questions that are most answered correctly.

If you have problems with questions and perform below 50%, you lack the fundamental knowledge necessary to pass the MBE.

When reviewing your answers to practice questions, it is essential to review all questions and answers, even those you got right.

Make sure you got that correct answer for the right reason.

Reviewing the questions and answers is critical for success on the exam.

Spend time reviewing those basic principles and working deliberately on the straightforward (and easy) questions that supplement learning.

Advice on using outlines

As a user of this governing law book, several of the following points are moot. They are included, so you can be confident that you are using the proper resources to prep for the bar.

Having a useful governing law study guide (such as this book) is critical.

Without effective resources, it is challenging to understand, learn and apply the governing law to the facts given in the question.

Some students use outlines that make learning difficult.

A few common mistakes about outlines:

- Learning outlines that are too long (e.g., more than 100 pages per subject) or too short (e.g., a seven-page Contracts outline). You will be overwhelmed by information or never learn enough governing law.

- Spending too much time comparing several outlines for the same subject.

  For example, using different Contracts outlines and needlessly comparing them. This confusion results in an undue focus on insignificant discrepancies.

- Outlining every subject. If you are not starting to study early, this consumes too much study time. Do not attempt to outline all subjects. It may be a good idea to outline a select few problematic subjects.

Using a detailed and well-organized governing law outline (e.g., this book) is essential; it saves time, organizes concepts, reduces anxiety, and helps you score well and pass the bar.

Easy questions make the difference

Limitations on the examiners lead to the first important insight into preparation for the exam – the kind of questions that decide whether you pass.

Performance on specific questions correlates with success or failure on the bar.

By analyzing statistics, questions predicting success or failure have been identified.

In general, the most challenging questions were not particularly good predictors of failure because most people who missed them passed the bar.

However, many of the straightforward questions were excellent predictors of success.

The median raw score ranges from about 60% to 66% correct on the MBE.

The National Conference of Bar Examiners (NCBE) writes, "expert panelists reported that they believed MBE items were generally easy, correctly estimating that about 66% of candidates would select the right answer to a typical item."

Depending on the exam's difficulty, in most states, scoring slightly below the median (miss up to 80 questions) still passes.

The most important questions to determine if you pass are not the exceedingly challenging ones but the easy ones where 90% of the examinees answer correctly.

The easy questions usually test a basic and regularly tested point of substantive law.

The wrong choices (i.e., the distracters) are typically easy to eliminate.

Your first task in preparing for the MBE is to get easy questions correct.

Study plan based upon statistics

These statistics show that an excellent performance on either the MBE questions (approximately 67% correct) or the state essays (4s on essays) assures you a passing score.

If you fail the MBE by 9 points or the essays by 5 points, the probability of passing the bar is in the single digits.

Put effort into performing well on the MBE questions for the following reasons.

- The questions are objective, and there are enough questions that are predictable concerning content and structure that it is possible, through reasonable effort, to answer 67% of the questions correctly.

- Studying the MBE first has the added advantage of preparing the necessary substantive law for state essays.

- The essays cover several subjects, the precise topic tested is unpredictable, and the answers are graded subjectively by graders who work quickly.

You had three years of law school practice with essays and less experience with multiple-choice questions.

Master the MBE before spending time preparing for the essays.

Factors associated with passing the bar

Based on an analysis of statistics from students' performance, the following factors predict the likelihood of passing the bar:

LSAT score

First-year Grade Point Average (GPA)

LSAT scores are a significant predictor of success on the bar because the LSAT requires similar multiple-choice test-taking skills as the MBE.

The LSAT tests many of the types of legal reasoning tested on the MBE.

A lower LSAT can be overcome by a comprehensive study of the MBE governing law, but these students must work harder.

Most of the subjects tested (e.g., constitutional law, civil procedure, contracts, criminal law, real property, torts) on the MBE are taken in the first year of law school.

First-year GPA measures mastery of subjects, preparedness for exams, and the ability to understand legal principles and apply them to given fact patterns.

The MBE measures the same factors but in a multiple-choice format instead of essays.

Pass rates based on GPA and LSAT scores

Past statistics indicate that law students with LSAT scores above 155 and a first-year GPA above 3.0 are reasonably assured of passing the bar.

They should study conscientiously and take practice MBEs to perform at the level needed, but they have little cause to panic.

Students with LSAT scores between 150 and 155 and a first-year GPA between 2.5 and 3.0 are in a bit more danger of failing and need to undertake rigorous preparation.

They must achieve a scaled score of 135 and take released practice exams and understand the reasons for incorrect choices. They should prepare for state essays by learning the governing laws in this book.

Students with LSAT scores between 145 and 150 and a first-year GPA between 2.2 and 2.5 have a moderate chance of passing the bar from deliberate efforts.

These students should not rely on ordinary commercial bar reviews and need intense training, particularly on the MBE component of the bar. They must devote 50-60 hours per week for seven weeks to prepare for the bar by learning the format and content of substantive law tested on the MBE. They should take released practice exams under exam conditions and conscientiously study the questions missed.

Students with LSAT scores below 145 and a GPA below 2.2 have had a failure rate of approximately 80%.

They must prep faithfully and conscientiously beyond the advice above and must engage in a rigorous course of study, more than is demanded by a traditional bar review course.

Notes for active learning

Learning and Applying the Substantive Law

Knowledge of substantive law

The fundamental reason for missing a question is 1) a failure to know the principle of law controlling the answer or 2) failure to understand how that principle is applied.

You must know and apply the governing law to pass the bar. If you do not know the governing law, you will not apply it to answer correctly.

Many students *think* they understand the governing law but do not know the nuances. Do not assume that you understand the governing (i.e., substantive) law. It is prevalent for students not to know the governing law well.

Re-learn the substantive and procedural law taught in first-year courses.

A major mistake is not to memorize the governing law outlined in this book.

The multiple-choice and essay portions test nuances and details of governing law. It is essential to analyze the governing law as it is applied in the context of the question.

On the multiple-choice section, many questions require fine-line distinctions between similar principles of law.

Several multiple-choice answers will *seem* correct, given the limited time to answer. If your knowledge of the governing law is suboptimal, you will not make these subtle distinctions and will have to guess on many questions.

For the essay to be developed, you must know the governing law and apply it to the issues within the call of the question.

If you do not know the governing law, you will not state the correct rule in your essay. You will be unable to apply the correct rule to the fact pattern.

Where to find the law

The questions must be related to the subject matter outlined in the bar examiners' (NCBE) materials.

While the NCBE outline is broad and ambiguous, years of experience with the exam delineate the scope of material you must learn.

The governing law covered in this book is foundational to the exam. The governing law statements were compiled by analyzing questions released by the multistate examiners. The analysis revealed a limited number of legal principles repeatedly tested.

Review these principles before taking practice exams and understand how they are applied to obtain the correct answer.

The property questions are probably the most difficult. The fact patterns are usually long and involve many parties in complex transactions.

In preparing for the exam, learn basic property principles and apply them. However, extensive studying into property law's crevices is not necessary to score well on these questions.

Feel confident that you do not have to go beyond the information provided in this book to find the governing law.

Controlling authority

The examiners have specified the sources of authority for the correct answers.

In Constitutional Law and Criminal Procedure, it is Supreme Court decisions.

In Criminal Law, it is common law.

In Evidence, the Federal Rules of Evidence controls.

In Torts and Property, it is the generally accepted view of United States law.

The UCC is the controlling authority in sales (Article 2) questions.

The NCBE released questions, and the published answers determine the controlling law through deduction.

Recent changes in the law

The exam is prepared months before it is given because of logistical requirements. Therefore, the examiners cannot incorporate recent changes in the law into the questions.

Recent changes in the law will not form the basis for correct answers.

If a recent change makes an answer initially designated as the correct answer to be incorrect, the examiners will credit more than one answer.

The recent holding of a Supreme Court case will not be tested for about two years since the decision was published.

Lesser-known issues and unusual applications

Some of the challenging exam questions are based on obscure principles of law.

Missing the most challenging questions will not cause you to fail the exam if you have a solid understanding of the governing law. You can learn these principles and answer the question correctly, thereby improving your overall performance.

There are instances where the correct answers are different from the usual rules.

For example, hearsay evidence inadmissible at trial is admissible before a judge hearing evidence on a preliminary question of fact (e.g., Federal Rules of Evidence 104(a)).

Practice applying the governing law

Some students know the governing law but have problems *applying* it to the facts.

The exam is as much about testing skills as it is about testing the governing law.

Therefore, knowledge of the governing law is not enough to pass.

You must practice answering multiple-choice questions and writing well-organized, coherent, and complete essays where you apply the governing law to the given facts.

Know which governing law is being tested

A typical wrong answer (i.e., distracter) on a question is an answer which is correct under a body of law other than the governing law being tested.

An example is a question governed by Article 2 of the Uniform Commercial Code (UCC), where an offer is irrevocable if:

1) it is in writing,

2) made by a merchant, and

3) states that it is irrevocable.

One of the wrong answers states the correct rule under the common law of contracts, where an offer is revocable unless consideration is paid (i.e., an option) for the promise to keep it open.

Answers which are always wrong

Some commonly used distracters are always wrong and can be eliminated quickly.

For example, a choice in an evidence question says, "character can only be attacked by reputation evidence." This choice is wrong because both opinion and reputation evidence is admissible under the Federal Rules of Evidence when character attacks are permissible.

Reading skills are critical. The basic level is reading to understand the facts, identify the issue and keep the parties distinct. A mistake at this juncture results in answering incorrectly, no matter how much law is known.

Understanding complex transactions

If the question involves a transaction with many parties, diagram the transaction before analyzing the choices.

The diagram should show the relationship between the parties (e.g., grantor-grantee, assignor-assignee), the transaction date, and the person's relationships in the transaction (e.g., donee, *bona fide* purchaser).

Impediments to careful reading

Two reasons candidates fail to read carefully are:

1) hurrying through a question,

2) fatigue due to a lack of sleep or strain caused by the exam.

A careful test taker maintains a steady, deliberate pace during the exam. Practice in advance and be well-rested on the test day.

Reading too much into a question

The examiners are committed to designing questions, which are "a fair index of whether the applicant has the ability to practice law." Psychometric experts ensure that they are fair and unbiased.

Even though you must read every word of these carefully drafted questions, do not read the question to find some bizarre interpretation.

The examiners must ask fair questions and not rely on "tricks." Reading too much into a question and looking for a trick lurking behind every fact leads to the wrong answer often.

It is the straightforward questions that determine whether you pass, not the occasional challenging question that tests some arcane principle of law.

Therefore, take questions at face value.

Read the call of the question first

Before reading the facts, read the call of the question because it indicates the task for selecting the correct answer. This perspective focuses your attention before reading the facts.

The question contains many *words of art*, such as "most likely," "best defense," or "least likely," which govern the correct answer.

The call is often phrased positively; the "best argument" or "most likely result."

Read answers for consistency with the question and eliminate inconsistent choices.

Negative calls

When the call of the question is negative, asking for the "weakest argument" or asking which of the options is "not" in a specified category, examine each option with the perspective that the choice with those negative characteristics is the correct answer.

After reading and understanding the question stem, read the call of the question again before reading the choices.

Analyze each choice with the requirements specified in the call of the question.

Read all choices

Never pick an answer until carefully reading all the choices. The objective is to pick the best answer, which cannot be determined until comparing the choices.

Sometimes the difference between the right and wrong answer is that one choice is more detailed or precisely sets forth the applicable law. You do not know that until reading all the answers carefully.

Broad statements of black letter law may be correct

When reading an answer, do not rule out choices with imprecise statements of the applicable *black letter* law.

If the examiners always included a choice that was precisely on point, the questions would be too easy. Instead, they often disguise the wording used in the correct answer.

For example, the Federal Rules of Evidence contain an elaborate set of relevancy rules that limit the right to introduce evidence of repairs after an accident. If there was a question where the introduction of that evidence was permissible, and no choices specifically cite the exception to the general rule of exclusion, an answer phrased with the general rule of relevancy "Admissible because its probative value outweighs its prejudicial effect," would be the correct answer.

Multiple-Choice Test-Taking Tactics

Determine the single correct answer

Increase the odds of picking the correct answer based on technical factors independent of substantive (governing) law knowledge.

The examiners' limitation is that every question must have one demonstrably correct and three demonstrably incorrect answers, limiting how the examiners write the choices.

From the question's construction, this limitation may give clues about the answer.

Process of elimination

Answering a multiple-choice question is not finding the ideal answer to the question asked but instead picking the best option.

Eliminate choices and evaluate the remaining choice for plausibility.

Eliminate choices that state an incorrect proposition of law or do not relate to the facts.

If you eliminate three options and the remaining one is acceptable, pick it and move on.

Elimination increases the odds

It takes about 125 correct answers to pass the MBE. An important strategy in reaching that number is intelligently eliminating choices.

If you are sure of the answer to only 50 of the 200 questions on the exam and confidently eliminate two of the four choices on the remaining 150 questions. Guess between the two remaining choices, and the odds predict 75 correct.

Those 75 correct, coupled with 50 questions you were confident of the answer, produce a raw score of 125 on the MBE and a scaled score above the benchmark 135.

Unfortunately, you cannot avoid guessing on questions, but intelligent methods reduce options to only two viable choices.

Sometimes you might not be able to eliminate the wrong answers just because you are sure of the answer to one of the choices. Eliminating with confidence even one choice increases the probability of correctly answering the question.

Eliminating two wrong answers

Specific questions on the MBE are challenging because of distinguishing between two choices when selecting the best answer.

A typical comment from examinees leaving the exam is, "I could not decide between the last two choices."

The positive side of that problem is eliminating two of the four choices.

Pick the winning side

The most common choice pattern is the "two-two" pattern – two choices state that the plaintiff prevails, and two that the defendant prevails.

The best approach for this type of question is to rely on your knowledge of the law or instinctive feeling to which conclusion is correct.

In a question with two choices on one side and two on the other side of a court's decision, first, pick a choice on the side you think should prevail.

Distinguish between the explanations following this conclusion and pick the choice that best justifies it.

Distance between choices on the other side

If the justifications following the conclusion for the side you chose seem indistinguishable, look at the explanations for the choices on the other side.

If the reasons for the choices on the other side are readily distinguishable, and one appears reasonable and the other incorrect, reconsider your initial conclusion.

Remember, the examiner is required to provide a distinguishable reason why one explanation of a general conclusion is correct, and the other is wrong.

That obligation does not exist if the general conclusion itself is incorrect.

Suppose choices (A) and (B) on one side look correct; that is, they are reasonable and consistent with the fact pattern. One of the choices with the opposite conclusion, answer (C), seems incorrect or inconsistent with the facts, and answer (D) with the same general conclusion sounds reasonable. From a strictly technical viewpoint, the best choice is answer (D).

Questions based upon a common fact pattern

There are several instances where two or more questions are based on the same facts.

Look at the second question's wording to guide the first question's correct answer. When asked to assume an answer to a first question from a fact pattern to answer the second question, the probability is high that the answer to the first question follows that assumption.

For example, if the first question has two choices beginning with "P prevails" and two with "D prevails," and the second question starts with "If P prevails," it is likely one of the "P prevails" choices is correct for the first question. If you picked "D prevails," think carefully before selecting it as the final answer.

Multiple true/false issues

In addition to true/false questions, the exam sometimes states three propositions in the root of the question and tests characteristics of those propositions in the call of the question.

The choices list various combinations of propositions.

The difference between this type of question and the double true/false question is that only four of the eight possible combinations fit into the options. It is possible to answer correctly even if you are not sure of all propositions' truth or falsity but are sure of one.

Correctly stated, but the inapplicable principle of law

The task of the examiners is to make the wrong choices look attractive. A creative way to accomplish this is to write a choice that impeccably states a rule of law that is not applicable because of facts in the root of the question.

For example, in a question where a person is an assignee, not a sublessee, one of the choices may correctly state the law for sublessees, but it is inapplicable to the fact pattern.

Therefore, these answer choices with inapplicable law can be confidently eliminated.

"Because" questions

Conjunctions are commonly used in the answers. It is essential to understand their role in determining whether a choice is correct.

The word "because" connects a conclusion and the reason for that conclusion with the facts in the body of the question.

There are two requirements for a question using "because" to be correct:

1) the conclusion must be correct,

2) the reasoning must logically follow based upon facts in the question, and the statement which follows "because" must be legally correct.

If the "because" choice has the correct result for the wrong reason, it is incorrect.

"If" questions

The conjunction "if" requires a much narrower focus than "because."

When a choice contains an "if," determine whether the entire statement is true, assuming that the proposition which follows the "if" is true.

There is no requirement that facts in the root of the question support the proposition following "if." There is no requirement for facts in the question to support the proposition that such a construction be reasonable.

"Because" or "if" need not be exclusive

There is no requirement for the conclusion following "if" or "because" to be exclusive.

For example, if a master could be liable in tort under the doctrine of *respondeat superior* or because the master was *negligent*, a choice using "if" or "because" holding the master liable would be correct if it stated either reason, even though the master might be liable for the other reason.

Exam tip for "because"

Notice that in an answer that would have been correct, the word "because" limits the facts you could consider to those in the body of the question containing specific facts.

The difference between the effect of "if" and "because" controls the answer.

Identify those limited situations (e.g., where the appropriate standard is strict liability) and distinguish them from those that are satisfactory (e.g., if the standard is negligence).

"Only if" requires exclusivity

Sometimes the words "only if" are used to distinguish between the two "affirmed" choices to make one wrong.

When an option uses the words "only if," assume that the entire proposition is correct as long as the words following "only if" are true.

The critical difference, where "only if" is used, is that the proposition cannot be true except when the condition is true. If there is another reason for the same result to be reached, the choice is wrong.

"Unless" questions

The conjunction "unless" has the same function as "only if," except that it precedes a negative exclusive condition instead of a positive exclusive condition.

It is essentially the mirror image of an "only if" choice.

For an option using "unless," reverse and substitute the words "only if" for "unless."

Limiting words

Choices can be made incorrect with limiting words that require that a proposition be true in all circumstances or under no circumstances.

Examples of limiting words include *all*, *any*, *never*, *always*, *only*, *every*, and *plenary*.

Making Correct Judgment Calls

Applying the law to the facts

Most questions give a fact pattern and ask which choice draws the correct legal conclusion required by the call of the question.

The first skill required is to draw inferences from facts given to place the conduct described in the question in the appropriate legal category.

The second skill is to apply the appropriate legal rule to conduct in that category and choose the option which reaches the appropriate conclusion.

The process of drawing inferences from a fact pattern and placing conduct in an appropriate category often requires judgment.

Bad judgment equals the wrong answer

To make the questions difficult, the examiners often place the conduct near the border of two different legal classifications.

Decide which side of the demarcation the conduct falls on. Inevitably, reasonable people can differ on these judgments.

If your judgment does not match the examiners, you will likely answer the question incorrectly, no matter how much law you know.

Mitigate this problem by reviewing released questions involving judgment calls where the examiners have published correct answers (i.e., their judgment call).

For example, a death occurring because the parties played Russian roulette is considered *depraved heart murder*, not *involuntary manslaughter*.

Judgment calls happen

Difficult judgment calls occur several times on the exam, and you are likely to make some close judgment calls incorrectly.

While this adds to the frustrations of multiple-choice tests, it is part of the exam.

By narrowing judgment call questions to two choices and guessing, you will get approximately half of them correct.

You will not fail the exam solely because you were unlucky on judgment calls.

The examiners remove many judgment calls by procedural devices.

The importance of procedure

The question may not ask what a jury should find on the facts.

The answer may be controlled by the procedural context of the criminal prosecution.

For example, it is given that the jury has found the defendant guilty of murder, and the only question on appeal is whether the judge should have granted a motion to dismiss at the end of hearing evidence. This is because a reasonable jury looking at the facts and inferences most favorable to the prosecution should not have found the defendant guilty of murder.

The same procedural issues exist when the question asks if a motion for summary judgment should be allowed or if the court should direct a verdict.

Exam Tips and Suggestions

Timing is everything

The time given to complete the exam is usually adequate if you practiced enough questions to improve speed and efficiency to the required level.

As you get closer to the test date, just doing practice questions is not enough.

You need to time your practice. Take previously released exams in two three-hour periods on the same day. Since these practice exams are approximately the same length as the exam, you will know if you have a timing problem.

If you do not practice under timed conditions, you risk exhausting time on the exam before answering all the questions.

Practice your timing under test-like conditions to know if the timing will be an issue. If you cannot complete the practice exam, you will have trouble with the exam.

If time is an issue, adjust your pace and continue practicing.

All questions do not require the same amount of time.

An approach for when time is not an issue

If you can complete 100 questions in three hours, use this strategy. At the start of the exam, break the allotted time into 15-minute intervals and write them down.

Set an initial pace of 9 questions every fifteen minutes.

Check your progress at each 15-minute interval.

If you completed 18 questions in the first half-hour, 36 in the first hour, 72 in the first two hours, and 90 in the first two and a half hours, you are on target to complete the exam on time. At this pace, you should complete 100 questions in two hours and forty-six minutes.

This leaves 14 minutes to check the answer sheet, revisit troublesome questions, or use the time to go a little slower on the last questions when fatigue impairs acuity.

If you find that your careful pace is faster than the budgeted 9 questions every 15 minutes, work at a faster pace, but use the extra time on the more challenging questions or in rechecking your work at the end.

Do *not* change the original answer choice unless you have a specific reason.

It is unwise to leave the exam early.

An approach for when time is an issue

During practice, continue answering questions to complete the section even after the time for self-paced exams has expired. Note which question you completed within the allocated time. Strive to complete the questions within the allotted time during your final exam prep.

If you learn from taking the practice test that you may not finish the questions in the allotted time on the actual exam, skip those questions with a long fact pattern followed by only one question. Keep your place on the answer sheet by skipping the row.

Return to those questions at the end and complete as many as time permits. Before turning your exam in, guess at the rest to reduce the number of random guesses.

Answer every question, even if you have not read the question, since wrong answers do *not* count against you.

Difficult questions

If you do not know the answer, do not spend a disproportionate amount of time on it since each question counts the same. Mark it in the test booklet, make a shrewd guess within the budgeted time and come back if time allows.

Do *not* leave questions unanswered. No points are deducted for wrong answers.

Minimize fatigue to maximize your score

The mental energy required to answer all the multiple-choice questions under stress produces fatigue (even with a lunch break).

Fatigue slows processing questions effectively and impairs reading comprehension. You may process questions more slowly at the end of each session and more quickly at the beginning before fatigue sets in.

Take at least two released exams under timed conditions to know how significantly fatigue affects your performance.

Be sure to arrive at the exam site on time. If necessary, stay at a nearby hotel rather than getting up early and risking a long drive the morning of the exam.

Relax during the lunch break and do not discuss the morning session with others.

You should know enough about your metabolism to eat the correct foods during the exam and reinforce appropriate caffeine levels if appropriate.

Proofread the answer sheet

As you decide on each correct answer, circle the corresponding letter in the exam book, and mark the appropriate block on the answer sheet.

The answer sheet is the only document graded by the examiners.

At the pace of 9 questions per 15 minutes, about 14 minutes should remain. Spend that time proofreading the answer sheet. Verify the answers circled to be certain that you marked the appropriate block on the answers.

Ensure that there are no blanks, and no questions have two answers.

Do *not* use this time to change an answer already selected unless you have a particularly good reason to change it.

If you have erased, ensure the erasure is thorough, or the computer may reject the answer because it cannot distinguish between marked answers.

If you have time after proofreading, review the problematic questions, and re-think the answers chosen. However, even after careful thought, hesitate to change an answer.

Do not leave any section of the exam early; use the allotted time wisely.

Intelligent preparation over a sustained period

There is no easy way to conquer an exam as challenging and comprehensive as the MBE, except through practice and an investment of time and effort well before the exam.

By diligently preparing, practicing questions, and intelligently assessing why questions were answered incorrectly, your skills for the exam will improve substantially.

Continue to improve those skills by following the advice given herein until reaching a proficiency level enabling you to pass the bar. This proficiency is accurately measured in multiple-choice format questions.

Some students will have to work harder to achieve the required proficiency.

The tools are in this study guide, and any law school graduate can be successful in passing the bar if they invest the required time and effort to be prepared.

Notes for active learning

Essay Preparation Strategies and Essay-Writing Suggestions

Memorize the law

Do not make the mistake of waiting too long before memorizing the governing law. Start learning the governing law early to be better prepared and pass the exam.

Memorize essential principles and focus on highly tested governing law.

Focus on the highly tested essay rules

Do not treat all subjects the same when you prepare for the essay portion of the exam.

Some governing law topics are tested more than others. It is crucial to focus on the highly tested topics (e.g., torts, contracts. property, civil procedure).

Know and apply enough governing laws to pass the bar – focus on commonly tested governing laws (e.g., negligence) provided in this book.

Practice writing essay answers each week

Practicing is crucial to a high score on essays. Practice regularly and avoid procrastination for this essential component of bar prep.

Incorporate practicing essay writing into your exam study schedule. To reduce procrastination, schedule time for writing practice essays each week.

For the MPT, practice by drafting full MPTs. Most examinees procrastinate on preparing for the MPT; there is nothing to memorize.

Do not make the *fatal mistake* of not practicing. The MPT portion is worth 20% of the UBE score.

Know the format and *practice that format to* increase your UBE score. This practice will increase your score and the probability of passing the bar.

Add one essay-specific subject each week

The Multistate Essay Exam (MEE) subjects include the 7 MBE subjects plus the 5 subjects of Business Associations (Agency, Partnerships, Corporations, and LLCs), Conflict of Laws, Family Law, Trusts and Estates, and Secured Transactions (UCC Article 9).

Combine highly tested subjects (e.g., torts) with less-tested subjects (e.g., secured transactions) and complex topics (e.g., contracts) with easier topics (e.g., business associations).

From preparation, know which subjects you struggle with and require a focused effort to master the essential governing law.

Make it easy for the grader to award points

Your answer to a question will probably be read in less than five minutes by a grader with a checklist to find that you have seen the issues and discussed them intelligently. Writing organized and clear answers makes it easy for the essay grader to award points.

Use headings for each of the major issues.

If the question suggests a structure for the answer because it is divided into parts or because the facts present a series of discrete issues, use the structure of the question, which is probably the structure of the checklist.

Use the IRAC method for the essay questions: state the issue, state the Rule. Apply the rule to the facts and conclude. IRAC seems simple, but following this approach makes it easier for the grader to know that you identified and addressed every issue and applied the law to the facts given.

IRAC results in more points during the exam.

Do not spend time trying to formulate eloquent issue statements. The question often outlines the issues, so an eloquent issue statement is redundant, and issue statements do not earn extra points.

Many examinees spend too much time developing an impressive issue statement and omit other essentials of their analysis (e.g., truncated analysis section).

An issue statement "Torts" or "Is the defendant liable for negligence?" is enough.

Do not waste time arguing both sides. There are no "two sides" for many essays to argue on bar essays because these are not law school essays.

Apply the law to facts and conclude unless asserting each party has good arguments.

Conclusion for each essay question

Points will be lost unless you conclude for each issue identified in the facts or are asked to address it in the call of the question.

Use caution starting the essay with the conclusion unless confident it is correct.

Many sample answers provided by the National Conference of Bar Examiners start with a definite and strong conclusion. Use caution to start with a conclusion unless confident (e.g., NCBE sample responses) your conclusion is correct.

Starting with a conclusion that is not correct draws attention to an incorrect conclusion at the start, which may influence the grader disproportionality. The grader may lose faith in your answer from the onset, and it is advisable to have a neutral heading rather than a firm conclusion that is wrong.

Tips for an easy-to-read essay

Use paragraph breaks between the Issue, Rule, Analysis, and Conclusion. Paragraph break makes it easy for the grader to read and score your essays. Additionally, this approach makes the answer appear longer and more complete.

Emphasize keywords and phrases. Underline key phrases so the grader notices that you addressed the governing law and applied it to the facts given.

After graders score several essays on the same topic, they scan essays for specific phrases that they expect to locate within a complete essay.

Think before you write

Read each question carefully to understand the facts and their necessary implications thoroughly and accurately.

After skimming the question, spend time on the focus line at the end of the question. Review the facts with the call of the question in mental focus.

Write a short outline of the issues raised. Outline in your mind the issues; state to yourself the tentative conclusions; test each conclusion from the standpoints of law and common sense; revise, as necessary.

Decide on a logical, orderly, and convincing arrangement for the response. Until then, you are not ready to write the answer.

Of the thirty-six minutes allotted to each essay, spend 15 minutes on issue spotting and organization and about twenty minutes writing the answer.

The ability to think and communicate like a lawyer

The Board knows that you have completed law school, under competent instructors, and have passed law school exams. The bar does not challenge the results of your law school courses.

The exam tests the ability to apply what you have learned to facts that might arise in practice and which, in some instances, involve several fields of law. The value of an answer depends not only on the correctness of the conclusions but on displaying essential legal principles and thinking like a lawyer.

Conclude on each issue presented. If a conclusion is derived from fuzzy facts, construct a well-reasoned argument supporting your conclusion to receive full credit regardless of if you conclude the same as the examiners.

If the correct answer depends on a provision of substantive law, which you are not familiar with, you can obtain a passing answer to the question by reaching a well-reasoned conclusion applying general law principles.

Do not try to limit the question to a particular subject area. Many questions combine traditional subjects, and you must be prepared to answer the question applying principles you learned across various subjects.

Do not restate the facts

The examiners know the facts; there is no time to waste. Do not restate the facts but use them to apply and integrate legal principles in writing the essay.

Do not fight the facts, particularly the focus line of the question.

For example, if the facts state that A executed a valid will, write about valid wills. If the question asks you to argue on behalf of A, do not argue on behalf of B because B has a prevailing argument. However, raise potential arguments which could be made on behalf of B and counter them in arguing on behalf of A.

Do not state abstract or irrelevant propositions of law

It is usually undesirable to begin an answer with a legal proposition. If the proposition is applicable, it will be more appropriate later to indicate the reason for your conclusion. If it is not applicable, do not state a surplus fact or legal principle.

Although it is seldom necessary to state an applicable rule of law in detail, make a sufficient reference to it so that the examiner appreciates your knowledge of the principle and conditions when it applies.

Do not, by speculating on different facts, nor in other ways, work into your answer some point of law with which you happen to be familiar, but which does not apply to the answer. Importantly, the examiners are not interested in knowing how many rules of law you know, but your ability to apply the applicable rules to the facts.

If the question says that A and B in the above hypothetical are unrelated, do not talk about the results which would occur if they were husband and wife.

Use the principles of law applicable to the call of the question and the facts. You must state the principles of applicable law to demonstrate to the examiner that you know the elements of the rule and how they apply to these facts.

For example, if the facts said that A transferred to B (a non-relative) the money necessary for B to purchase Blackacre from C and asks who owns Blackacre, you would say, "Since A furnished the consideration for the purchase of Blackacre and B took the title to the property in their name, B holds title to Blackacre in a resulting trust for A.

Do not detail the black letter law of resulting trusts since you have shown your knowledge by properly applying the facts to the law of resulting trusts.

Do not fight the facts and address a contrary fact not presented. The examiners may take points away if you make that mistake because you are not focused on the issues presented.

Discuss all the issues raised

A grasp of all the issues is essential.

For example, if there are three issues in a question, a discussion of only one issue, no matter how masterly, if coupled with omitting the others, could not result in 100% credit. It would probably result in a score of 33%.

The exam includes many issues in most questions so it can be graded mechanically. This maintains consistency across a group of several graders for each exam question.

The grader has a checklist of issues and awards most points for the examinee that identifies issues and intelligently discusses each.

Failure to see and discuss enough issues intelligently is probably the biggest reason for failure on the essay portion of the exam.

Methods for finding all issues

Use all the facts presented. Failure to discuss facts probably means that you missed important issues.

If you must decide in the early part of the question (e.g., does the court have jurisdiction) and you decide that issue so the remaining facts become irrelevant, make an alternative assumption ("If the court does have jurisdiction") and answer the question in the alternative using facts which would otherwise be irrelevant.

Do not avoid issues because you are not sure of the substantive law. If the examiners stated that X's nephew helped X escape after a crime, discuss the nephew's status as an accessory after the fact. If you do not know whether he is a close enough relative to be exempt under the statute, answer this issue by making alternative assumptions.

Indicators requiring alternative arguments

Ambiguous terms – if there are words in the fact pattern that are neutral or ambiguous such as "put up," the examiners look for possible interpretations of these terms.

Language in quotes – language placed in quotes is almost always ambiguous and must be construed as part of the answer.

Avoid ambiguous, rambling statements and verbosity

Generally, do not use compound sentences. Two separate sentences are preferred.

Complex sentences are particularly useful to apply the facts of the question to the applicable principle of law.

For example, in the previous resulting trust hypothetical, write, "Since B purchased Blackacre and took title in their name with money furnished by A, A holds title to Blackacre in a resulting trust, even if B has not signed a memorandum."

Avoid undue repetition

If the same principle of law and conclusion apply to two parts of an answer, state it once in detail, and refer back for the second part.

For example, if you have discussed A's liability and now must discuss B's liability, say, "B is also guilty of murder for the same reasons as A. (see discussion above)."

Avoid slang and colloquialism

The examiners judge your formal writing style.

If the examiner shows humor with names and events, do not show your sense of humor.

Use the standard abbreviations:

P for Plaintiff

D for Defendant

K for Contract

BFP for *Bona Fide* purchaser

Write legibly and coherently

Printing is usually easier to read than handwriting.

Use all the pages, and do not crowd your answer.

Plan your answer so that you do not have to use inserts and arrows.

Timing strategies

On the MEE, you must complete six equally weighted essay questions in three hours; an average of 30 minutes per question.

You have flexibility with time limitations as questions are not of the same difficulty.

There are two absolute figures:

spend no more than 45 minutes on any question,

spend at least 20 minutes on each question.

Be careful about not going over the time limit on the first question because this will require a readjustment of your timing for the entire session. If you miss the deadlines, re-divide your remaining time so that you will have an equal amount of time on each question.

If you go over by 15 minutes a question, do not allocate 30 minutes for other questions.

Stay focused

Do not start by reading the entire exam. Answer the questions in order and do not consider more than one question at a time.

After answering, put it out of your mind and not worry about your response. Keep your mind clear to focus on the next question.

Proofread your answers as time permits.

Law school essay grading matrix

An "A" answer is an outstanding response. It correctly and fully identifies dispositive issues and sub-issues raised by the question. The answer states the applicable legal rules and sub-rules with precision. It analyzes the question thoroughly with the applicable rules and explores alternative analysis where appropriate. It applies the law to the facts to conclude and is not cluttered by irrelevant matters. An "A" answer demonstrates an objectively superior mastering of the subject. An answer is not an "A" answer simply because it is better than most students' answers.

A "B" answer is a good response. It presents the four components of a good answer (issues, rules, analysis & application, and conclusion), but it does so in a way that could be improved. For example, it may be that not all critical issues have been spotted, or the issues are not presented clearly. The statement of legal rules captures that basic law but may not develop the law's complexities or nuances. The analysis is competent but lacks subtlety and may be somewhat simplistic or conclusory.

A "C" answer is a minimally competent response. It contains the four components of a good answer (issues, rules, analysis & application, and conclusion) but may not distinguish them. Perhaps only some issues have been identified while others are missed. The rules of law lack completeness or accuracy. The analysis and application may be shallow and conclusory. Conclusions may be questionable and not well-defended.

A "D" answer lacks basic components. It may identify the wrong issues or none. Rules are stated incorrectly. The analysis is conclusory or absent. The law is not applied to the facts coherently. Conclusions are unsupported or missing. The response exhibits a lack of knowledge of legal issues and rules or demonstrates an inability to engage in legal analysis

Best wishes with your preparation!

Appendix

Overview of American Law

Overview of American Law

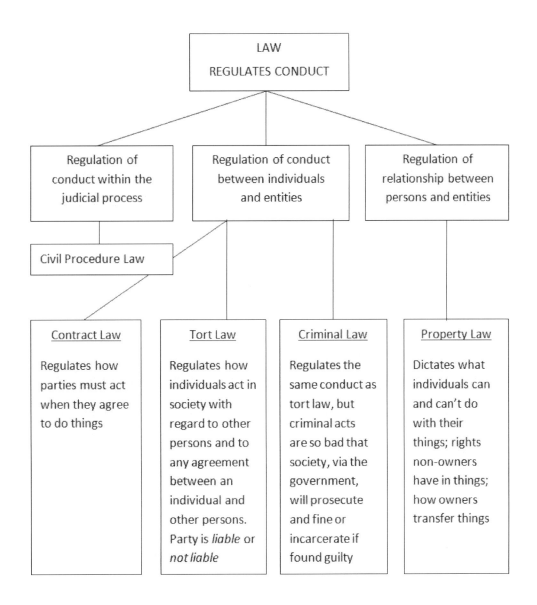

U.S. Court Systems – Federal and State Courts

There are two kinds of courts in the USA – federal courts and state courts.

Federal courts are established under the U.S. Constitution by Congress to decide disputes involving the Constitution and laws passed by Congress. A state establishes state and local courts (within states, local courts are established by cities, counties, and other municipalities).

Jurisdiction of federal and state courts

The differences between federal courts and state courts are defined by jurisdiction.[1] Jurisdiction refers to the kinds of cases that a particular court is authorized to hear and adjudicate (i.e., the pronouncement of a legally binding judgment upon the parties to the dispute).

Federal court jurisdiction is limited to the types of cases listed in the Constitution and specifically provided by Congress. For the most part, federal courts only hear:

- cases in which the United States is a party[2];

- cases involving violations of the U.S. Constitution or federal laws (under federal-question jurisdiction[3]);

- cases between citizens of different states if the amount in controversy *exceeds* $75,000 (under diversity jurisdiction[4]); and

- bankruptcy, copyright, patent, and maritime law cases.

State courts, in contrast, have broad jurisdiction, so the cases individual citizens are likely to be involved in (e.g., robberies, traffic violations, contracts, and family disputes) are usually heard and decided in state courts. The only cases state courts are not allowed to hear are lawsuits against the United States and those involving certain specific federal laws: criminal, antitrust, bankruptcy, patent, copyright, and some maritime law cases.

In many cases, both federal and state courts have jurisdiction whereby the plaintiff (i.e., the party initiating the suit) can choose whether to file their claim in state or federal court.

Criminal cases involving federal laws can be tried only in federal court, but most criminal cases involve violations of state law and are tried in state court. Robbery is a crime, but what law makes it is a crime? Except for certain exceptions, state laws, not federal laws, make robbery a crime. There are only a few federal laws about robbery, such as the law that makes it a federal crime to rob a bank whose deposits are insured by a federal agency. Examples of other federal crimes are the transport of illegal drugs into the country or across state lines and using the U.S. mail system to defraud consumers.

Crimes committed on federal property (e.g., national parks or military reservations) are prosecuted in federal court.

Federal courts may hear cases concerning state laws if the issue is whether the state law violates the federal Constitution. Suppose a state law forbids slaughtering animals outside of certain limited areas. A neighborhood association brings a case in state court against a defendant who sacrifices chickens in their backyard. When the court issues an order (i.e., an injunction[5]) forbidding the defendant from further sacrifices, the defendant challenges the state law in federal court as an unconstitutional infringement of religious freedom.

Some conduct is illegal under both federal and state laws. For example, federal laws prohibit employment discrimination, and the states have added additional legal restrictions. A person can file their claim in either federal or state court under federal law or federal and state laws. A case that only involves a state law can be brought only in state court.

Appeals for review of actions by federal administrative agencies are federal civil cases.

For example, if the Environmental Protection Agency, over the objection of area residents, issued a permit to a paper mill to discharge water used in its milling process into the Scenic River, the residents may appeal and have the federal court of appeals review the agency's decision.

---

[1] *jurisdiction* – 1) the legal authority of a court to hear and decide specific types of case; 2) the geographic area over which the court has the authority to decide cases.

[2] *parties* – the plaintiff and the defendant in a lawsuit.

[3] *federal-question jurisdiction* – the federal district courts' authorization to hear and decide cases arising under the Constitution, laws, or treaties of the United States.

[4] *diversity jurisdiction* – the federal district courts' authority to hear and decide civil cases involving plaintiffs and defendants who are citizens of different states (or U.S. citizens and foreign nationals) and meet specific statutory requirements.

[5] *injunction* – a judge's order that a party takes or refrain from taking a particular action. An injunction may be preliminary until the outcome of a case is determined or permanent.

Organization of the federal courts

Congress has divided the country into 94 federal judicial districts, with each having a U.S. district court. The U.S. district courts are the federal trial courts -- where federal cases are tried, witnesses testify, and juries serve.

Each district has a U.S. bankruptcy court, which is part of the district court that administers the U.S. bankruptcy laws.

Congress uses state boundaries to help define the districts. Some districts cover an entire state, like Idaho. Other districts cover just part of a state, like the Northern District of California. Congress placed each of the ninety-four districts in one of twelve regional circuits whereby each circuit has a court of appeals. The losing party can petition the court of appeals to review the case to determine if the district judge applied the law correctly.

There is a U.S. Court of Appeals for the Federal Circuit, whose jurisdiction is defined by subject matter rather than geography. It hears appeals from certain courts and agencies, such as the U.S. Court of International Trade, the U.S. Court of Federal Claims, and the U.S. Patent and Trademark Office, and certain types of cases from the district courts (mainly lawsuits claiming that patents have been infringed).

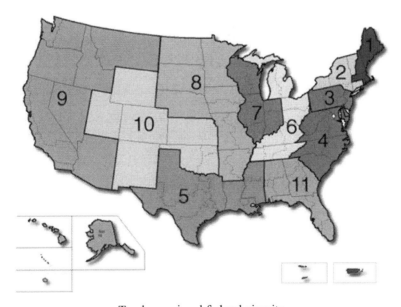

Twelve regional federal circuits

The Supreme Court in Washington, D.C., is the highest court in the nation. The losing party can petition in a case in the court of appeals (or, sometimes, in a state supreme court), can petition the Supreme Court to hear an appeal.

Unlike a court of appeals, the Supreme Court does not have to hear the case. The Supreme Court hears only a small percentage of the cases it is asked to review.

Notes for active learning

How Civil Cases Move Through the Federal Courts

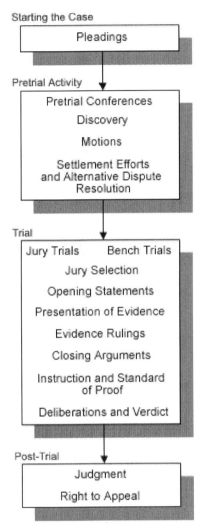

A federal civil case begins when a person, or their legal representative, files a paper with the clerk of the court that asserts another person's wrongful act injured the person. In legal terminology, the plaintiff files a *complaint* against the defendant.

The defendant files an *answer* to the complaint. These written statements of the party's positions are called pleadings. In some circumstances, the defendant may file a *motion* instead of an answer; the motion asks the court to take some action, such as dismiss the case or require the plaintiff to explain more clearly what the lawsuit is about.

Jury trials

In a jury trial, the jury decides what happened, and to apply the legal standards, the judge tells them to apply to reach a verdict. The plaintiff presents evidence supporting its view of the case, and the defendant presents evidence rebutting the plaintiff's evidence or supporting its view of the case. From these presentations, the jury must decide what happened and applied the law to those facts.

The jury never decides what law applies to the case; that is the role of the judge. For example, in a discrimination case where the plaintiff alleged that their workplace was hostile, the judge tells the jury the legal standard for a hostile environment.

The jury would have to decide whether the plaintiff's description of events was true and whether those events met the legal standard. A trial jury, or petit jury, may consist of six to twelve jurors in a civil case.

Bench trials

If the parties agree not to have a *jury trial* and leave the fact-finding to the judge, the trial is a *bench trial*. In bench and jury trials, the judge ensures the correct legal standards are followed.

In contrast to a jury trial, the judge decides the facts and renders the verdict in a *bench trial*.

For example, in a discrimination case in which the plaintiff alleged a hostile environment, the judge would determine the legal standard for a hostile environment and decide whether the plaintiff's description of events was true and whether those events met the legal standard.

Some kinds of cases always have bench trials. For example, there is never a jury trial if the plaintiff is seeking an injunction, an order from the judge that the defendant does, or stop doing something, as opposed to monetary damages.

Some statutes provide that a judge must decide the facts in certain types of cases.

Jury selection

A jury trial begins with the selection of jurors. Citizens are selected for jury service through a process set out in laws passed by Congress and in the federal rules of procedure.

First, citizens are called to court to be available to serve on juries. These citizens are selected at random from sources, in most districts, lists of registered voters, which may be augmented by other sources, such as lists of licensed drivers in the judicial district.

The judge and the lawyers choose who will serve on the jury.

To choose the jurors, the judge and sometimes the lawyers ask prospective jurors questions to determine if they will decide the case fairly, a process known as *voir dire*.

The lawyers may request that the judge excuse jurors they think may not be impartial, such as those who know a party in the case or who have had an experience that might make them favor one side over the other. These requests for rejecting jurors are *challenges for cause*.

The lawyers may request that the judge excuse a certain number of jurors without reason; these requests are *peremptory challenges*.

Instructions and standard of proof

Following the closing arguments, the judge gives instructions to the jury, explaining the relevant law, how the law applies to the case, and what questions the jury must decide.

How sure do jurors have to be before they reach a verdict? One important instruction the judge gives the jury is the standard of proof they must follow in deciding the case.

The courts, through their decisions, and Congress, through statutes, have established standards by which facts must be proven in criminal and civil cases.

In civil cases, to decide for the plaintiff, the jury must determine by a *preponderance of the evidence* that the defendant failed to perform a legal duty and violated the plaintiff's rights. A preponderance of the evidence means that, based on the evidence, the evidence favors the plaintiff more (even if only slightly) than it favors the defendant.

If the evidence in favor of the plaintiff could be placed on one side of a scale and that in favor of the defendant on the other, the plaintiff would win if the evidence in favor of the plaintiff was heavy enough to tip the scale. If the two sides were even, or if the scale tipped for the defendant, the defendant would win.

Judgment

In civil cases, if the jury (or judge) decides in favor of the plaintiff, the result usually is that the defendant must pay the plaintiff money or damages. The judge orders the defendant to pay the decided amount. Sometimes the defendant is ordered to take some specific action that will restore the plaintiff's rights. If the defendant wins the case, there is nothing more the trial court needs to do as the case is disposed of and the defendant is held not liable.

Right to appeal

The losing party in a federal civil case has a right to appeal the verdict to the U.S. court of appeals (i.e., Federal Circuit Courts) and ask the court to review the case to determine whether the trial was conducted properly. The losing party in the state trial court has a right to appeal the verdict to the state court of appeal.

The grounds for appeal usually are that the federal district (or state) judge made an error, either in the procedure (e.g., admitting improper evidence) or interpreting the law. The government may appeal in civil cases, as any other party may. Neither party may appeal if there was no trial -- parties settled their civil case out of court.

Notes for active learning

How Criminal Cases Move Through the Federal Courts

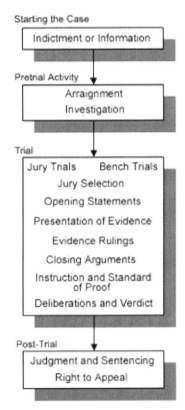

Indictment or information

A criminal case formally begins with an indictment or information, which is a formal accusation that a person committed a crime.

An indictment may be obtained when a lawyer (i.e., prosecutor) for the executive branch of the U.S. government (i.e., U.S. attorney or assistant U.S. attorney) present evidence to a federal grand jury that, according to the government, indicates a person committed a crime.

The U.S. attorney tries to convince the grand jury that there is enough evidence to show that the person probably committed the crime and should be formally accused. If the grand jury agrees, it issues an indictment.

A grand jury is different from a trial jury or petit jury.

A grand jury determines whether the person may be tried for a crime; a petit jury listens to the evidence presented at the trial and determines whether the defendant is guilty.

Petit is French for "small"; petit juries usually consist of twelve jurors in criminal cases.

Grand is French for "large"; grand juries have from sixteen to twenty-three jurors.

Grand jury indictments are most often used for *felonies* (i.e., punishable by imprisonment of more than a year or by death) such as bank robberies or sales of illegal drugs.

Grand jury indictments are not necessary to prosecute *misdemeanors* (i.e., less serious than a felony but more serious than an infraction) and are necessary for felonies.

For lesser crimes, the U.S. attorney issues an *information* that substitutes for an indictment. For example, speeding on a highway in a national park is a misdemeanor.

An information is used when a defendant waives an indictment by a grand jury.

Arraignment

After the grand jury issues the indictment, the accused (i.e., defendant) is summoned to court or arrested (if not already in custody). The next step is an arraignment, a proceeding in which the defendant is brought before a judge, told of the charges they are accused of, and asked to plead guilty or not guilty. If the defendant's plea is guilty, a time is set for the defendant to return to court to be sentenced.

If the defendant pleads "not guilty," the time is set for the trial.

A defendant may enter a plea bargain with the prosecution--usually by agreeing to plead guilty to some but not all charges or lesser charges. The prosecution drops the remaining charges.

About nine out of ten defendants in criminal cases plead guilty.

Investigation

In a criminal case, a defense lawyer conducts a thorough investigation before trial, interviewing witnesses, visiting the crime scene, and examining physical evidence. An important part of this investigation is determining whether the evidence the government plans to use to prove its case was obtained legally.

The Fourth Amendment to the Constitution forbids unreasonable searches and seizures. To enforce this protection, the Supreme Court has decided that illegally seized evidence cannot be used at trial for most purposes.

For example, if the police seize evidence from a defendant's home without a search warrant, the lawyer for the defendant can ask the court to exclude the evidence from use at trial. The court holds a hearing to determine whether the search was unreasonable.

If the court rules that key evidence was seized illegally and cannot be used, the government often drops the charges against the defendant.

If the government has a strong case and the court ruled that the evidence was obtained legally, the defendant may decide to plead guilty rather than go to trial, where a conviction is likely.

Deliberations and verdict

After receiving its instructions from the judge, the jury retires to the jury room to discuss the evidence and reach a verdict (a decision on the factual issues). A criminal jury verdict must be unanimous; all jurors must agree that the defendant is guilty or not guilty.

If the jurors cannot agree, the judge declares a mistrial, and the prosecutor must decide whether to ask the court to dismiss the case or have it presented to another jury.

Judgment and sentencing

In federal criminal cases, if the jury (or judge, if there is no jury) decides that the defendant is guilty, the judge sets a date for a sentencing hearing. In federal criminal cases, the jury does not decide whether the defendant will go to prison or for how long; the judge does.

In federal death penalty cases, the jury does decide whether the defendant will receive a death sentence. Sentencing statutes passed by Congress control the judge's sentencing decision. Additionally, judges use Sentencing Guidelines, issued by the U.S. Sentencing Commission, as a source of advice as to the proper sentence. The guidelines consider the nature of the offense and the offender's criminal history.

A presentence report, prepared by one of the court's probation officers, provides the judge with information about the offender and the offense, including the sentence recommended by the guidelines. After determining the sentence, the judge signs a judgment, including the plea, the verdict, and sentence.

Right to appeal

A defendant who is found guilty in a federal criminal trial has a right to appeal the decision to the U.S. court of appeals, that is, ask the court of appeals to review the case to determine whether the trial was conducted properly. The grounds for appeal are usually that the district judge is said to have made an error, either in a procedure (admitting improper evidence, for example) or interpreting the law.

A defendant who pled guilty may not appeal the conviction.

A defendant who pled guilty may have the right to appeal their sentence.

The government may not appeal if a defendant in a criminal case is found not guilty because the Double Jeopardy Clause of the Fifth Amendment to the Constitution provides that no person shall "be twice put in jeopardy of life or limb" for the same offense.

This reflects society's belief that, even if a subsequent trial might finally find a defendant guilty, it is not proper for the government to harass an acquitted defendant through repeated retrials.

However, the government may sometimes appeal a sentence.

Notes for active learning

How Civil and Criminal Appeals Move Through the Federal Courts

Assignment of Judges

Alternative Dispute Resolution (ADR)

Review of Lower Court Decision

Oral Argument

Decision

The Supreme Court of the United States

Assignment of judges

The courts of appeals usually assign cases to a panel of three judges. The panel decides the case for the entire court. Sometimes, when the parties request it or a question of unusual importance, the judges on the appeals court assemble *en banc* (a rare event).

Review of a lower court decision

In making its decision, the panel reviews key parts of the record. The record consists of the documents filed in the case at trial and the transcript of the trial proceedings. The panel learns about the lawyers' legal arguments from the lawyers' briefs.

Briefs are written documents that each side submits to explain its case and tell why the court should decide in its favor.

Oral argument

If the court permits oral argument, the lawyers for each side have a limited amount of time (typically between 15 to 30 minutes) to argue (i.e., advocate and explain) their case to the judges (or justices at the highest court in the jurisdiction) in a formal courtroom session. The judges (or justices for the highest court in the jurisdiction) frequently question the attorneys about the relevant law as it applies to the facts and issues in the case before them.

A court of appeals differs from the federal trial courts. There are no jurors, witnesses, or court reporters. The lawyers for each side, but not the parties, are usually present in the courtroom.

Decision

After the submission of briefs and oral arguments, the judges discuss the case privately, consider relevant *precedents* (court decisions from higher courts in prior cases with similar facts and legal issues), and reach a decision. Courts are required to follow precedents.

For example, a U.S. court of appeals must follow the U.S. Supreme Court's decisions; a district court must follow the decisions of the U.S. Supreme Court and the decisions of the court of appeals of its circuit.

Courts are influenced by decisions they are not required to follow, such as the decisions of other circuits. Courts follow precedent unless they set forth reasons for the diversion.

At least two of the three judges on the panel must agree on a decision. One judge who agrees with the decision is chosen to write an opinion, which announces and explains the decision.

If a judge on the panel disagrees with the majority's opinion, the judge may write a dissent, giving reasons for disagreeing.

Many appellate opinions are published in books of opinions, called reporters. The opinions are read carefully by other judges and lawyers looking for precedents to guide them in their cases.

The accumulated judicial opinions make up a body of law known as *case law*, which is usually an accurate predictor of how future cases will be decided.

For decisions that the judges believe are important to the parties and contribute little to the law, the appeals courts frequently use short, unsigned opinions that often are not published.

If the court of appeals decides that the trial judge incorrectly interpreted the law or followed incorrect procedures, it reverses the district court's decision.

For example, the court of appeals could hold that the district judge allowed the jury to base its decision on evidence that never should have been admitted, and thus the defendant cannot be guilty.

Most of the time, courts of appeals uphold, rather than the reverse, district court decisions.

Sometimes when a higher court reverses the decision of the district court, it sends the case back (i.e., *remand* the case) to the lower court for another trial.

For example, *Miranda v. Arizona* case (1966), the Supreme Court ruled 5-4 that Ernesto Miranda's confession could not be used as evidence because he had not been advised of his right to remain silent or of his right to have a lawyer present during questioning.

However, the government did have other evidence against him. The case was remanded for a new trial, in which the improperly obtained confession was not used as evidence, but the other evidence convicted Miranda.

The Supreme Court of the United States

The Supreme Court is the highest in the nation. It is a different kind of appeals court; its major function is not correcting errors made by trial judges but clarifying the law in cases of national importance or when lower courts disagree about interpreting the Constitution or federal laws.

The Supreme Court does not have to hear every case that it is asked to review. Each year, losing parties ask the Supreme Court to review about 8,000 cases.

Almost all cases come to the Court as a *petition for writ of certiorari*. The court selects only about 80 to 120 of the most significant cases to review with oral arguments.

Supreme Court decisions establish a precedent for interpreting the Constitution and federal laws; holdings that state and federal courts must follow.

The power of judicial review makes the Supreme Court's role in our government vital. Judicial review is the power of a court when deciding a case to declare that a law passed by a legislature or action by the executive branch is invalid because it is inconsistent with the Constitution.

Although district courts, courts of appeals, and state courts can exercise the power of judicial review, their decisions about federal law are always subject, on appeal, to review by the Supreme Court.

When the Supreme Court declares a law unconstitutional, its decision can only be overruled by a later decision of the Supreme Court or Amendment to the Constitution.

Seven of the twenty-seven Amendments to the Constitution have invalidated the decisions of the Supreme Court. However, most Supreme Court cases do not concern the constitutionality of laws, but the interpretation of laws passed by Congress.

Although Congress has steadily increased the number of district and appeals court judges over the years, the Supreme Court has remained the same size since 1869. It consists of a Chief Justice and eight associate justices.

Like the federal court of appeals and federal district judges, the Supreme Court justices are appointed by the President with the Senate's *advice and consent*.

Unlike the judges in the courts of appeals, Supreme Court justices never sit on panels. Absent recusal, nine justices hear cases, and a majority ruling decides cases.

The Supreme Court begins its annual session, or term, on the first Monday of October. The term lasts until the Court has announced its decisions in cases where it has heard an argument that term—usually late June or early July.

During the term, the Court, sitting for two weeks at a time, hears oral arguments on Monday through Wednesday and holds private conferences to discuss the cases, reach decisions, and begin preparing the written opinions that explain its decisions.

Most decisions and opinions are released in the late spring and early summer.

Standards of review for federal courts

Standard of review	De novo	Clearly erroneous	Abuse of discretion
Type of decision under review	Question of the law	Question of fact	Discretionary action
Lower-court decision maker	Trial judge	Trial judge	Trial judge
Deference given to lower court	No deference	Substantial deference	Extreme deference
Party typically benefitted	Appellant	Appellee	Appellee
Definition	An appellate court reviews the legal question anew and independently, without regard to the conclusions reached by the trial court. "When *de novo* review is compelled, no form of appellate deference is acceptable." *Salve Regina College v. Russell*, (1991).	A finding is 'clearly erroneous' when although there is evidence to support it, the reviewing court on the entire evidence is left with the definite and firm conviction that a mistake has been committed. *United States v. United States Gypsum Co.*, (1948) "If the district court's account of the evidence is plausible in light of the record viewed in its entirety, the court of appeals may not reverse it even though convinced that had it been sitting as the trier of fact, it would have weighed the evidence differently. When there are two permissible views of the evidence, the factfinder's choice between them cannot be clearly erroneous." *Anderson v. Bessemer City*, (1985).	Generally, an abuse of discretion only occurs where no reasonable person could take the view adopted by the trial court. If reasonable persons could differ, no abuse of discretion can be found. *Harrington v. DeVito*, (7th Cir. 1981) Under the abuse of discretion standard, a trial court's decision will not be disturbed unless the appellate court has a definite and firm conviction that the lower court made a clear error of judgment or exceeded the bounds of permissible choice in the circumstances. We will not alter a trial court's decision unless it can be shown that the court's decision was an arbitrary, capricious, whimsical, or manifestly unreasonable judgment. *Wright v. Abbott Laboratories, Inc.*, (10th Cir. 2001)
Examples	Motions for summary judgment, constitutional questions, statutory interpretation	Questions regarding who did what, where, and when; questions of intent and motive; questions of ultimate fact (such as negligence)	Rule 11 sanctions, attorney's fees, courtroom management, motions to compel, injunctions, and temporary restraining orders.

The Constitution of the United States (*a transcription*)

THE U.S. NATIONAL ARCHIVES & RECORDS ADMINISTRATION
www.archives.gov

The following text is a transcription of the Constitution as it was inscribed by Jacob Shallus on parchment (the document on display in the Rotunda at the National Archives Museum.) The spelling and punctuation reflect the original.

The Constitution of the United States: A Transcription

The following text is a transcription of the Constitution as it was inscribed by Jacob Shallus on parchment (displayed in the Rotunda at the National Archives Museum.) The authenticated text of the Constitution can be found on the website of the Government Printing Office.

We the People of the United States, in Order to form a more perfect Union, establish Justice, insure domestic Tranquility, provide for the common defence, promote the general Welfare, and secure the Blessings of Liberty to ourselves and our Posterity, do ordain and establish this Constitution for the United States of America.

Article. I

Section. 1.

All legislative Powers herein granted shall be vested in a Congress of the United States, which shall consist of a Senate and House of Representatives.

Section. 2.

The House of Representatives shall be composed of Members chosen every second Year by the People of the several States, and the Electors in each State shall have the Qualifications requisite for Electors of the most numerous Branch of the State Legislature.

No Person shall be a Representative who shall not have attained to the Age of twenty five Years, and been seven Years a Citizen of the United States, and who shall not, when elected, be an Inhabitant of that State in which he shall be chosen.

Representatives and direct Taxes shall be apportioned among the several States which may be included within this Union, according to their respective Numbers, which shall be determined by adding to the whole Number of free Persons, including those bound to Service for a Term of Years, and excluding Indians not taxed, three fifths of all other Persons. The actual Enumeration shall be made within three Years after the first Meeting of the Congress of the United States, and within every subsequent Term of ten Years, in such Manner as they shall by Law direct. The Number of Representatives shall not exceed one for every thirty Thousand, but each State shall have at Least one Representative; and until such enumeration shall be made, the State of New Hampshire shall be entitled to chuse three, Massachusetts eight, Rhode-Island and Providence

---

Plantations one, Connecticut five, New-York six, New Jersey four, Pennsylvania eight, Delaware one, Maryland six, Virginia ten, North Carolina five, South Carolina five, and Georgia three.

When vacancies happen in the Representation from any State, the Executive Authority thereof shall issue Writs of Election to fill such Vacancies.

The House of Representatives shall chuse their Speaker and other Officers; and shall have the sole Power of Impeachment.

Section. 3.

The Senate of the United States shall be composed of two Senators from each State, chosen by the Legislature thereof, for six Years; and each Senator shall have one Vote.

Immediately after they shall be assembled in Consequence of the first Election, they shall be divided as equally as may be into three Classes. The Seats of the Senators of the first Class shall be vacated at the Expiration of the second Year, of the second Class at the Expiration of the fourth Year, and of the third Class at the Expiration of the sixth Year, so that one third may be chosen every second Year; and if Vacancies happen by Resignation, or otherwise, during the Recess of the Legislature of any State, the Executive thereof may make temporary Appointments until the next Meeting of the Legislature, which shall then fill such Vacancies.

No Person shall be a Senator who shall not have attained to the Age of thirty Years, and been nine Years a Citizen of the United States, and who shall not, when elected, be an Inhabitant of that State for which he shall be chosen.

The Vice President of the United States shall be President of the Senate, but shall have no Vote, unless they be equally divided.

The Senate shall chuse their other Officers, and also a President pro tempore, in the Absence of the Vice President, or when he shall exercise the Office of President of the United States.

The Senate shall have the sole Power to try all Impeachments. When sitting for that Purpose, they shall be on Oath or Affirmation. When the President of the United States is tried, the Chief Justice shall preside: And no Person shall be convicted without the Concurrence of two thirds of the Members present.

Judgment in Cases of Impeachment shall not extend further than to removal from Office, and disqualification to hold and enjoy any Office of honor, Trust or Profit under the United States: but the Party convicted shall nevertheless be liable and subject to Indictment, Trial, Judgment and Punishment, according to Law.

Section. 4.

The Times, Places and Manner of holding Elections for Senators and Representatives, shall be prescribed in each State by the Legislature thereof; but the Congress may at any time by Law make or alter such Regulations, except as to the Places of chusing Senators.

The Congress shall assemble at least once in every Year, and such Meeting shall be on the first Monday in December, unless they shall by Law appoint a different Day.

Section. 5.

Each House shall be the Judge of the Elections, Returns and Qualifications of its own Members, and a Majority of each shall constitute a Quorum to do Business; but a smaller Number may adjourn from day to day, and may be authorized to compel the Attendance of absent Members, in such Manner, and under such Penalties as each House may provide.

Each House may determine the Rules of its Proceedings, punish its Members for disorderly Behaviour, and, with the Concurrence of two thirds, expel a Member.

Each House shall keep a Journal of its Proceedings, and from time to time publish the same, excepting such Parts as may in their Judgment require Secrecy; and the Yeas and Nays of the Members of either House on any question shall, at the Desire of one fifth of those Present, be entered on the Journal.

Neither House, during the Session of Congress, shall, without the Consent of the other, adjourn for more than three days, nor to any other Place than that in which the two Houses shall be sitting.

Section. 6.

The Senators and Representatives shall receive a Compensation for their Services, to be ascertained by Law, and paid out of the Treasury of the United States. They shall in all Cases, except Treason, Felony and Breach of the Peace, be privileged from Arrest during their Attendance at the Session of their respective Houses, and in going to and returning from the same; and for any Speech or Debate in either House, they shall not be questioned in any other Place.

No Senator or Representative shall, during the Time for which he was elected, be appointed to any civil Office under the Authority of the United States, which shall have been created, or the Emoluments whereof shall have been encreased during such time; and no Person holding any Office under the United States, shall be a Member of either House during his Continuance in Office.

Section. 7.

All Bills for raising Revenue shall originate in the House of Representatives; but the Senate may propose or concur with Amendments as on other Bills.

Every Bill which shall have passed the House of Representatives and the Senate, shall, before it become a Law, be presented to the President of the United States; If he approves he shall sign it, but if not he shall return it, with his Objections to that House in which it shall have originated, who shall enter the Objections at large on their Journal, and proceed to reconsider it. If after such Reconsideration two thirds of that House shall agree to pass the Bill, it shall be sent, together with the Objections, to the other House, by which it shall likewise be reconsidered, and if approved by two thirds of that House, it shall become a Law. But in all such Cases the Votes of both Houses shall be determined by yeas and Nays, and the Names of the Persons voting for and against the Bill shall be entered on the Journal of each House respectively. If any Bill shall not be returned by the President within ten Days (Sundays excepted) after it shall have been presented to him, the Same shall be a Law, in like Manner as if he had signed it, unless the Congress by their Adjournment prevent its Return, in which Case it shall not be a Law.

Every Order, Resolution, or Vote to which the Concurrence of the Senate and House of Representatives may be necessary (except on a question of Adjournment) shall be presented to the President of the United States; and before the Same shall take Effect, shall be approved by him, or being disapproved by him, shall be repassed by two thirds of the Senate and House of Representatives, according to the Rules and Limitations prescribed in the Case of a Bill.

Section. 8.

The Congress shall have Power To lay and collect Taxes, Duties, Imposts and Excises, to pay the Debts and provide for the common Defence and general Welfare of the United States; but all Duties, Imposts and Excises shall be uniform throughout the United States;

To borrow Money on the credit of the United States;

To regulate Commerce with foreign Nations, and among the several States, and with the Indian Tribes;

To establish an uniform Rule of Naturalization, and uniform Laws on the subject of Bankruptcies throughout the United States;

To coin Money, regulate the Value thereof, and of foreign Coin, and fix the Standard of Weights and Measures;

To provide for the Punishment of counterfeiting the Securities and current Coin of the United States;

To establish Post Offices and post Roads;

To promote the Progress of Science and useful Arts, by securing for limited Times to Authors and Inventors the exclusive Right to their respective Writings and Discoveries;

To constitute Tribunals inferior to the Supreme Court;

To define and punish Piracies and Felonies committed on the high Seas, and Offences against the Law of Nations;

To declare War, grant Letters of Marque and Reprisal, and make Rules concerning Captures on Land and Water;

To raise and support Armies, but no Appropriation of Money to that Use shall be for a longer Term than two Years;

To provide and maintain a Navy;

To make Rules for the Government and Regulation of the land and naval Forces;

To provide for calling forth the Militia to execute the Laws of the Union, suppress Insurrections and repel Invasions;

To provide for organizing, arming, and disciplining, the Militia, and for governing such Part of them as may be employed in the Service of the United States, reserving to the States respectively, the Appointment of the Officers, and the Authority of training the Militia according to the discipline prescribed by Congress;

To exercise exclusive Legislation in all Cases whatsoever, over such District (not exceeding ten Miles square) as may, by Cession of particular States, and the Acceptance of Congress, become the Seat of the Government of the United States, and to exercise like Authority over all Places purchased by the Consent of the Legislature of the State in which the Same shall be, for the Erection of Forts, Magazines, Arsenals, dock-Yards, and other needful Buildings;—And

To make all Laws which shall be necessary and proper for carrying into Execution the foregoing Powers, and all other Powers vested by this Constitution in the Government of the United States, or in any Department or Officer thereof.

Section. 9.

The Migration or Importation of such Persons as any of the States now existing shall think proper to admit, shall not be prohibited by the Congress prior to the Year one thousand eight hundred and eight, but a Tax or duty may be imposed on such Importation, not exceeding ten dollars for each Person.

The Privilege of the Writ of Habeas Corpus shall not be suspended, unless when in Cases of Rebellion or Invasion the public Safety may require it.

No Bill of Attainder or ex post facto Law shall be passed.

No Capitation, or other direct, Tax shall be laid, unless in Proportion to the Census or enumeration herein before directed to be taken.

No Tax or Duty shall be laid on Articles exported from any State.

No Preference shall be given by any Regulation of Commerce or Revenue to the Ports of one State over those of another: nor shall Vessels bound to, or from, one State, be obliged to enter, clear, or pay Duties in another.

No Money shall be drawn from the Treasury, but in Consequence of Appropriations made by Law; and a regular Statement and Account of the Receipts and Expenditures of all public Money shall be published from time to time.

No Title of Nobility shall be granted by the United States: And no Person holding any Office of Profit or Trust under them, shall, without the Consent of the Congress, accept of any present, Emolument, Office, or Title, of any kind whatever, from any King, Prince, or foreign State.

Section. 10.

No State shall enter into any Treaty, Alliance, or Confederation; grant Letters of Marque and Reprisal; coin Money; emit Bills of Credit; make any Thing but gold and silver Coin a Tender in Payment of Debts; pass any Bill of Attainder, ex post facto Law, or Law impairing the Obligation of Contracts, or grant any Title of Nobility.

No State shall, without the Consent of the Congress, lay any Imposts or Duties on Imports or Exports, except what may be absolutely necessary for executing it's inspection Laws: and the net

Produce of all Duties and Imposts, laid by any State on Imports or Exports, shall be for the Use of the Treasury of the United States; and all such Laws shall be subject to the Revision and Controul of the Congress.

No State shall, without the Consent of Congress, lay any Duty of Tonnage, keep Troops, or Ships of War in time of Peace, enter into any Agreement or Compact with another State, or with a foreign Power, or engage in War, unless actually invaded, or in such imminent Danger as will not admit of delay.

Article. II

Section. 1.

The executive Power shall be vested in a President of the United States of America. He shall hold his Office during the Term of four Years, and, together with the Vice President, chosen for the same Term, be elected, as follows

Each State shall appoint, in such Manner as the Legislature thereof may direct, a Number of Electors, equal to the whole Number of Senators and Representatives to which the State may be entitled in the Congress: but no Senator or Representative, or Person holding an Office of Trust or Profit under the United States, shall be appointed an Elector.

The Electors shall meet in their respective States, and vote by Ballot for two Persons, of whom one at least shall not be an Inhabitant of the same State with themselves. And they shall make a List of all the Persons voted for, and of the Number of Votes for each; which List they shall sign and certify, and transmit sealed to the Seat of the Government of the United States, directed to the President of the Senate. The President of the Senate shall, in the Presence of the Senate and House of Representatives, open all the Certificates, and the Votes shall then be counted. The Person having the greatest Number of Votes shall be the President, if such Number be a Majority of the whole Number of Electors appointed; and if there be more than one who have such Majority, and have an equal Number of Votes, then the House of Representatives shall immediately chuse by Ballot one of them for President; and if no Person have a Majority, then from the five highest on the List the said House shall in like Manner chuse the President. But in chusing the President, the Votes shall be taken by States, the Representation from each State having one Vote; A quorum for this Purpose shall consist of a Member or Members from two thirds of the States, and a Majority of all the States shall be necessary to a Choice. In every Case, after the Choice of the President, the Person having the greatest Number of Votes of the Electors shall be the Vice President. But if there should remain two or more who have equal Votes, the Senate shall chuse from them by Ballot the Vice President.

The Congress may determine the Time of chusing the Electors, and the Day on which they shall give their Votes; which Day shall be the same throughout the United States.

No Person except a natural born Citizen, or a Citizen of the United States, at the time of the Adoption of this Constitution, shall be eligible to the Office of President; neither shall any Person be eligible to that Office who shall not have attained to the Age of thirty five Years, and been fourteen Years a Resident within the United States.

In Case of the Removal of the President from Office, or of his Death, Resignation, or Inability to discharge the Powers and Duties of the said Office, the Same shall devolve on the Vice President, and the Congress may by Law provide for the Case of Removal, Death, Resignation or Inability, both of the President and Vice President, declaring what Officer shall then act as President, and such Officer shall act accordingly, until the Disability be removed, or a President shall be elected.

The President shall, at stated Times, receive for his Services, a Compensation, which shall neither be encreased nor diminished during the Period for which he shall have been elected, and he shall not receive within that Period any other Emolument from the United States, or any of them.

Before he enters on the Execution of his Office, he shall take the following Oath or Affirmation:—"I do solemnly swear (or affirm) that I will faithfully execute the Office of President of the United States, and will to the best of my Ability, preserve, protect and defend the Constitution of the United States."

Section. 2.

The President shall be Commander in Chief of the Army and Navy of the United States, and of the Militia of the several States, when called into the actual Service of the United States; he may require the Opinion, in writing, of the principal Officer in each of the executive Departments, upon any Subject relating to the Duties of their respective Offices, and he shall have Power to grant Reprieves and Pardons for Offences against the United States, except in Cases of Impeachment.

He shall have Power, by and with the Advice and Consent of the Senate, to make Treaties, provided two thirds of the Senators present concur; and he shall nominate, and by and with the Advice and Consent of the Senate, shall appoint Ambassadors, other public Ministers and Consuls, Judges of the supreme Court, and all other Officers of the United States, whose Appointments are not herein otherwise provided for, and which shall be established by Law: but the Congress may by Law vest the Appointment of such inferior Officers, as they think proper, in the President alone, in the Courts of Law, or in the Heads of Departments.

The President shall have Power to fill up all Vacancies that may happen during the Recess of the Senate, by granting Commissions which shall expire at the End of their next Session.

Section. 3.

He shall from time to time give to the Congress Information of the State of the Union, and recommend to their Consideration such Measures as he shall judge necessary and expedient; he may, on extraordinary Occasions, convene both Houses, or either of them, and in Case of Disagreement between them, with Respect to the Time of Adjournment, he may adjourn them to such Time as he shall think proper; he shall receive Ambassadors and other public Ministers; he shall take Care that the Laws be faithfully executed, and shall Commission all the Officers of the United States.

Section. 4.

The President, Vice President and all civil Officers of the United States, shall be removed from Office on Impeachment for, and Conviction of, Treason, Bribery, or other high Crimes and Misdemeanors.

Article III

Section. 1.

The judicial Power of the United States, shall be vested in one supreme Court, and in such inferior Courts as the Congress may from time to time ordain and establish. The Judges, both of the supreme and inferior Courts, shall hold their Offices during good Behaviour, and shall, at stated Times, receive for their Services, a Compensation, which shall not be diminished during their Continuance in Office.

Section. 2.

The judicial Power shall extend to all Cases, in Law and Equity, arising under this Constitution, the Laws of the United States, and Treaties made, or which shall be made, under their Authority;—to all Cases affecting Ambassadors, other public Ministers and Consuls;—to all Cases of admiralty and maritime Jurisdiction;—to Controversies to which the United States shall be a Party;—to Controversies between two or more States;—between a State and Citizens of another State,—between Citizens of different States,—between Citizens of the same State claiming Lands under Grants of different States, and between a State, or the Citizens thereof, and foreign States, Citizens or Subjects.

In all Cases affecting Ambassadors, other public Ministers and Consuls, and those in which a State shall be Party, the supreme Court shall have original Jurisdiction. In all the other Cases before mentioned, the supreme Court shall have appellate Jurisdiction, both as to Law and Fact, with such Exceptions, and under such Regulations as the Congress shall make.

The Trial of all Crimes, except in Cases of Impeachment, shall be by Jury; and such Trial shall be held in the State where the said Crimes shall have been committed; but when not committed within any State, the Trial shall be at such Place or Places as the Congress may by Law have directed.

Section. 3.

Treason against the United States, shall consist only in levying War against them, or in adhering to their Enemies, giving them Aid and Comfort. No Person shall be convicted of Treason unless on the Testimony of two Witnesses to the same overt Act, or on Confession in open Court.

The Congress shall have Power to declare the Punishment of Treason, but no Attainder of Treason shall work Corruption of Blood, or Forfeiture except during the Life of the Person attainted.

Article. IV

Section. 1.

Full Faith and Credit shall be given in each State to the public Acts, Records, and judicial Proceedings of every other State. And the Congress may by general Laws prescribe the Manner in which such Acts, Records and Proceedings shall be proved, and the Effect thereof.

Section. 2.

The Citizens of each State shall be entitled to all Privileges and Immunities of Citizens in the several States.

A Person charged in any State with Treason, Felony, or other Crime, who shall flee from Justice, and be found in another State, shall on Demand of the executive Authority of the State from which he fled, be delivered up, to be removed to the State having Jurisdiction of the Crime.

No Person held to Service or Labour in one State, under the Laws thereof, escaping into another, shall, in Consequence of any Law or Regulation therein, be discharged from such Service or Labour, but shall be delivered up on Claim of the Party to whom such Service or Labour may be due.

Section. 3.

New States may be admitted by the Congress into this Union; but no new State shall be formed or erected within the Jurisdiction of any other State; nor any State be formed by the Junction of two or more States, or Parts of States, without the Consent of the Legislatures of the States concerned as well as of the Congress.

The Congress shall have Power to dispose of and make all needful Rules and Regulations respecting the Territory or other Property belonging to the United States; and nothing in this Constitution shall be so construed as to Prejudice any Claims of the United States, or of any particular State.

Section. 4.

The United States shall guarantee to every State in this Union a Republican Form of Government, and shall protect each of them against Invasion; and on Application of the Legislature, or of the Executive (when the Legislature cannot be convened), against domestic Violence.

Article. V

The Congress, whenever two thirds of both Houses shall deem it necessary, shall propose Amendments to this Constitution, or, on the Application of the Legislatures of two thirds of the several States, shall call a Convention for proposing Amendments, which, in either Case, shall be valid to all Intents and Purposes, as Part of this Constitution, when ratified by the Legislatures of three fourths of the several States, or by Conventions in three fourths thereof, as the one or the other Mode of Ratification may be proposed by the Congress; Provided that no Amendment which may be made prior to the Year One thousand eight hundred and eight shall in any Manner affect the first and fourth Clauses in the Ninth Section of the first Article; and that no State, without its Consent, shall be deprived of its equal Suffrage in the Senate.

Article. VI

All Debts contracted and Engagements entered into, before the Adoption of this Constitution, shall be as valid against the United States under this Constitution, as under the Confederation.

This Constitution, and the Laws of the United States which shall be made in Pursuance thereof; and all Treaties made, or which shall be made, under the Authority of the United States, shall be the supreme Law of the Land; and the Judges in every State shall be bound thereby, any Thing in the Constitution or Laws of any State to the Contrary notwithstanding.

The Senators and Representatives before mentioned, and the Members of the several State Legislatures, and all executive and judicial Officers, both of the United States and of the several States, shall be bound by Oath or Affirmation, to support this Constitution; but no religious Test shall ever be required as a Qualification to any Office or public Trust under the United States.

Article. VII

The Ratification of the Conventions of nine States, shall be sufficient for the Establishment of this Constitution between the States so ratifying the Same.

The Word, "the," being interlined between the seventh and eighth Lines of the first Page, The Word "Thirty" being partly written on an Erazure in the fifteenth Line of the first Page, The Words "is tried" being interlined between the thirty second and thirty third Lines of the first Page and the Word "the" being interlined between the forty third and forty fourth Lines of the second Page.

Attest William Jackson Secretary, done in Convention by the Unanimous Consent of the States present the Seventeenth Day of September in the Year of our Lord one thousand seven hundred and Eighty seven and of the Independance of the United States of America the Twelfth In witness whereof We have hereunto subscribed our Names, G°. Washington, *Presidt and deputy from Virginia*

Delaware
Geo: Read
Gunning Bedford jun
John Dickinson
Richard Bassett
Jaco: Broom

Maryland
James McHenry
Dan of St Thos.
Jenifer
Danl. Carroll

Virginia
John Blair
James Madison Jr.

North Carolina
Wm. Blount
Richd. Dobbs
Spaight
Hu Williamson

South Carolina
J. Rutledge
Charles Cotesworth
Pinckney
Charles Pinckney
Pierce Butler

Georgia
William Few
Abr Baldwin

New Hampshire
John Langdon
Nicholas Gilman

Massachusetts
Nathaniel Gorham
Rufus King

Connecticut
Wm. Saml. Johnson
Roger Sherman

New York
Alexander Hamilton

New Jersey
Wil: Livingston
David Brearley
Wm. Paterson
Jona: Dayton

Pensylvania
B Franklin
Thomas Mifflin
Robt. Morris
Geo. Clymer
Thos. FitzSimons
Jared Ingersoll
James Wilson
Gouv Morris

Enactment of the Bill of Rights of the United States of America (1791)

The first ten Amendments to the Constitution make up the Bill of Rights. Written by James Madison in response to calls from several states for greater constitutional protection for individual liberties, the Bill of Rights lists specific prohibitions on governmental power. The Virginia Declaration of Rights, written by George Mason, strongly influenced Madison.

One of the contention points between Federalists and Anti-Federalists was the Constitution's lack of a bill of rights that would place specific limits on government power.

Federalists argued that the Constitution did not need a bill of rights because the people and the states kept powers not explicitly given to the federal government.

Anti-Federalists held that a *bill of rights* was necessary to safeguard individual liberty.

Madison, then a member of the U.S. House of Representatives, went through the Constitution itself, making changes where he thought most appropriate.

Several Representatives, led by Roger Sherman, objected that Congress had no authority to change the wording of the Constitution. Therefore, Madison's changes were presented as a list of amendments that would follow Article VII.

The House approved 17 amendments. Of these 17, the Senate approved 12. Those 12 were sent to the states for approval in August of 1789. Of those 12 proposed amendments, 10 were quickly ratified. Virginia's legislature became the last to ratify the Amendments on December 15, 1791. These Amendments are the Bill of Rights.

The Bill of Rights is a list of limits on government power. For example, what the Founders saw as the natural right of individuals to speak and worship freely was protected by the First Amendment's prohibitions on Congress from making laws establishing a religion or abridging freedom of speech.

Another example is the natural right to be free from the government's unreasonable intrusion in one's home was safeguarded by the Fourth Amendment's warrant requirements.

Other precursors to the Bill of Rights include English documents such as the Magna Carta[1], the Petition of Rights, the English Bill of Rights, and the Massachusetts Body of Liberties.

The Magna Carta illustrates Compact Theory[1] as well as initial strides toward limited government. Its provisions address individual rights and political rights. Latin for "Great Charter," the Magna Carta was written by Barons in Runnymede, England, and forced on the King.

Although the protections were generally limited to the prerogatives of the Barons, the Magna Carta embodied the general principle that the King accepted limitations on his rule. These included the fundamental acknowledgment that the king was not above the law.

Included in the Magna Carta are protections for the English church, petitioning the king, freedom from the forced quarter of troops and unreasonable searches, due process and fair trial protections, and freedom from excessive fines. These protections can be found in the First, Third, Fourth, Fifth, Sixth, and Eighth Amendments to the Constitution.

The Magna Carta is the oldest compact in England. The Mayflower Compact, the Fundamental Orders of Connecticut, and the Albany Plan are examples from the American colonies.

The Articles of Confederation was a compact among the states, and the Constitution creates a compact based on a federal system between the national government, state governments, and the people. The Hayne-Webster Debate focused on the compact created by the Constitution.

---

[1] Philosophers including Thomas Hobbes, John Locke, and Jean-Jacques Rousseau theorized that peoples' condition in a "state of nature" (that is, outside of society) is one of freedom, but that freedom inevitably degrades into war, chaos, or debilitating competition without the benefit of a system of laws and government. They reasoned, therefore, that for their happiness, individuals willingly trade some of their natural freedom in exchange for the protections provided by the government.

The Bill of Rights: Amendments I–X

Amendment I

Congress shall make no law respecting an establishment of religion, or prohibiting the free exercise thereof; or abridging the freedom of speech, or of the press; or the right of the people peaceably to assemble, and to petition the government for a redress of grievances.

Amendment II

A well regulated militia, being necessary to the security of a free state, the right of the people to keep and bear arms, shall not be infringed.

Amendment III

No soldier shall, in time of peace be quartered in any house, without the consent of the owner, nor in time of war, but in a manner to be prescribed by law.

Amendment IV

The right of the people to be secure in their persons, houses, papers, and effects, against unreasonable searches and seizures, shall not be violated, and no warrants shall issue, but upon probable cause, supported by oath or affirmation, and particularly describing the place to be searched, and the persons or things to be seized.

Amendment V

No person shall be held to answer for a capital, or otherwise infamous crime, unless on a presentment or indictment of a grand jury, except in cases arising in the land or naval forces, or in the militia, when in actual service in time of war or public danger; nor shall any person be subject for the same offense to be twice put in jeopardy of life or limb; nor shall be compelled in any criminal case to be a witness against himself, nor be deprived of life, liberty, or property, without due process of law; nor shall private property be taken for public use, without just compensation.

Amendment VI

In all criminal prosecutions, the accused shall enjoy the right to a speedy and public trial, by an impartial jury of the state and district wherein the crime shall have been committed, which district shall have been previously ascertained by law, and to be informed of the nature and cause of the accusation; to be confronted with the witnesses against him; to have compulsory process for obtaining witnesses in his favor, and to have the assistance of counsel for his defense.

Amendment VII

In suits at common law, where the value in controversy shall exceed twenty dollars, the right of trial by jury shall be preserved, and no fact tried by a jury, shall be otherwise reexamined in any court of the United States, than according to the rules of the common law.

Amendment VIII

Excessive bail shall not be required, nor excessive fines imposed, nor cruel and unusual punishments inflicted.

Amendment IX

The enumeration in the Constitution, of certain rights, shall not be construed to deny or disparage others retained by the people.

Amendment X

The powers not delegated to the United States by the Constitution, nor prohibited by it to the states, are reserved to the states respectively, or to the people.

Constitutional Amendments XI–XXVII

AMENDMENT XI

Passed by Congress March 4, 1794. Ratified February 7, 1795.

Note: Article III, section 2, of the Constitution was modified by amendment 11.

The Judicial power of the United States shall not be construed to extend to any suit in law or equity, commenced or prosecuted against one of the United States by Citizens of another State, or by Citizens or Subjects of any Foreign State.

AMENDMENT XII

Passed by Congress December 9, 1803. Ratified June 15, 1804.

Note: A portion of Article II, section 1 of the Constitution was superseded by the 12th amendment.

The Electors shall meet in their respective states and vote by ballot for President and Vice-President, one of whom, at least, shall not be an inhabitant of the same state with themselves; they shall name in their ballots the person voted for as President, and in distinct ballots the person voted for as Vice-President, and they shall make distinct lists of all persons voted for as President, and of all persons voted for as Vice-President, and of the number of votes for each, which lists they shall sign and certify, and transmit sealed to the seat of the government of the United States, directed to the President of the Senate; -- the President of the Senate shall, in the presence of the Senate and House of Representatives, open all the certificates and the votes shall then be counted; -- The person having the greatest number of votes for President, shall be the President, if such number be a majority of the whole number of Electors appointed; and if no person have such majority, then from the persons having the highest numbers not exceeding three on the list of those voted for as President, the House of Representatives shall choose immediately, by ballot, the President. But in choosing the President, the votes shall be taken by states, the representation from each state having one vote; a quorum for this purpose shall consist of a member or members from two-thirds of the states, and a majority of all the states shall be necessary to a choice. [And if the House of Representatives shall not choose a President whenever the right of choice shall devolve upon them, before the fourth day of March next following, then the Vice-President shall act as President, as in case of the death or other constitutional disability of the President. --]* The person having the greatest number of votes as Vice-President, shall be the Vice-President, if such number be a majority of the whole number of Electors appointed, and if no person have a majority, then from the two highest numbers on the list, the Senate shall choose the Vice-President; a quorum for the purpose shall consist of two-thirds of the whole number of Senators, and a majority of the whole number shall be necessary to a choice. But no person constitutionally ineligible to the office of President shall be eligible to that of Vice-President of the United States.

Superseded by section 3 of the 20th Amendment.

AMENDMENT XIII

Passed by Congress January 31, 1865. Ratified December 6, 1865.

Note: A portion of Article IV, section 2, of the Constitution was superseded by the 13th amendment.

Section 1.

Neither slavery nor involuntary servitude, except as a punishment for crime whereof the party shall have been duly convicted, shall exist within the United States, or any place subject to their jurisdiction.

Section 2.

Congress shall have power to enforce this article by appropriate legislation.

AMENDMENT XIV

Passed by Congress June 13, 1866. Ratified July 9, 1868.

Note: Article I, section 2, of the Constitution was modified by section 2 of the 14th amendment.

Section 1.

All persons born or naturalized in the United States, and subject to the jurisdiction thereof, are citizens of the United States and of the State wherein they reside. No State shall make or enforce any law which shall abridge the privileges or immunities of citizens of the United States; nor shall any State deprive any person of life, liberty, or property, without due process of law; nor deny to any person within its jurisdiction the equal protection of the laws.

Section 2.

Representatives shall be apportioned among the several States according to their respective numbers, counting the whole number of persons in each State, excluding Indians not taxed. But when the right to vote at any election for the choice of electors for President and Vice-President of the United States, Representatives in Congress, the Executive and Judicial officers of a State, or the members of the Legislature thereof, is denied to any of the male inhabitants of such State, being twenty-one years of age,* and citizens of the United States, or in any way abridged, except for participation in rebellion, or other crime, the basis of representation therein shall be reduced in the proportion which the number of such male citizens shall bear to the whole number of male citizens twenty-one years of age in such State.

Section 3.

No person shall be a Senator or Representative in Congress, or elector of President and Vice-President, or hold any office, civil or military, under the United States, or under any State, who, having previously taken an oath, as a member of Congress, or as an officer of the United States, or as a member of any State legislature, or as an executive or judicial officer of any State, to support the Constitution of the United States, shall have engaged in insurrection or rebellion against the same, or given aid or comfort to the enemies thereof. But Congress may by a vote of two-thirds of each House, remove such disability.

Section 4.

The validity of the public debt of the United States, authorized by law, including debts incurred for payment of pensions and bounties for services in suppressing insurrection or rebellion, shall not be questioned. But neither the United States nor any State shall assume or pay any debt or obligation incurred in aid of insurrection or rebellion against the United States, or any claim for the loss or emancipation of any slave; but all such debts, obligations and claims shall be held illegal and void.

Section 5.

The Congress shall have the power to enforce, by appropriate legislation, the provisions of this article.

*Changed by section 1 of the 26th Amendment.

AMENDMENT XV

Passed by Congress February 26, 1869. Ratified February 3, 1870.

Section 1.

The right of citizens of the United States to vote shall not be denied or abridged by the United States or by any State on account of race, color, or previous condition of servitude.

Section 2.

The Congress shall have the power to enforce this article by appropriate legislation.

AMENDMENT XVI

Passed by Congress July 2, 1909. Ratified February 3, 1913.

Note: Article I, section 9, of the Constitution was modified by amendment 16.

The Congress shall have power to lay and collect taxes on incomes, from whatever source derived, without apportionment among the several States, and without regard to any census or enumeration.

AMENDMENT XVII

Passed by Congress May 13, 1912. Ratified April 8, 1913.

Note: Article I, section 3, of the Constitution was modified by the 17th Amendment.

The Senate of the United States shall be composed of two Senators from each State, elected by the people thereof, for six years; and each Senator shall have one vote. The electors in each State shall have the qualifications requisite for electors of the most numerous branch of the State legislatures.

When vacancies happen in the representation of any State in the Senate, the executive authority of such State shall issue writs of election to fill such vacancies: *Provided*, That the legislature of any State may empower the executive thereof to make temporary appointments until the people fill the vacancies by election as the legislature may direct.

This amendment shall not be so construed as to affect the election or term of any Senator chosen before it becomes valid as part of the Constitution.

AMENDMENT XVIII

Passed by Congress December 18, 1917. Ratified January 16, 1919. Repealed by Amendment 21.

Section 1.

After one year from the ratification of this article the manufacture, sale, or transportation of intoxicating liquors within, the importation thereof into, or the exportation thereof from the United States and all territory subject to the jurisdiction thereof for beverage purposes is hereby prohibited.

Section 2.

The Congress and the several States shall have concurrent power to enforce this article by appropriate legislation.

Section 3.

This article shall be inoperative unless it shall have been ratified as an amendment to the Constitution by the legislatures of the several States, as provided in the Constitution, within seven years from the date of the submission hereof to the States by the Congress.

AMENDMENT XIX

Passed by Congress June 4, 1919. Ratified August 18, 1920.

The right of citizens of the United States to vote shall not be denied or abridged by the United States or by any State on account of sex.

Congress shall have power to enforce this article by appropriate legislation.

AMENDMENT XX

Passed by Congress March 2, 1932. Ratified January 23, 1933.

Note: Article I, section 4, of the Constitution was modified by section 2 of this Amendment. In addition, a portion of the 12th Amendment was superseded by section 3.

Section 1.

The terms of the President and the Vice President shall end at noon on the 20th day of January, and the terms of Senators and Representatives at noon on the 3d day of January, of the years in which such terms would have ended if this article had not been ratified; and the terms of their successors shall then begin.

Section 2.

The Congress shall assemble at least once in every year, and such meeting shall begin at noon on the 3d day of January, unless they shall by law appoint a different day.

Section 3.

If, at the time fixed for the beginning of the term of the President, the President elect shall have died, the Vice President elect shall become President. If a President shall not have been chosen before the time fixed for the beginning of his term, or if the President elect shall have failed to qualify, then the Vice President elect shall act as President until a President shall have qualified; and the Congress may by law provide for the case wherein neither a President elect nor a Vice President elect shall have qualified, declaring who shall then act as President, or the manner in which one who is to act shall be selected, and such person shall act accordingly until a President or Vice President shall have qualified.

Section 4.

The Congress may by law provide for the case of the death of any of the persons from whom the House of Representatives may choose a President whenever the right of choice shall have devolved upon them, and for the case of the death of any of the persons from whom the Senate may choose a Vice President whenever the right of choice shall have devolved upon them.

Section 5.

Sections 1 and 2 shall take effect on the 15th day of October following the ratification of this article.

Section 6.

This article shall be inoperative unless it shall have been ratified as an amendment to the Constitution by the legislatures of three-fourths of the several States within seven years from the date of its submission.

AMENDMENT XXI

Passed by Congress February 20, 1933. Ratified December 5, 1933.

Section 1.

The eighteenth article of amendment to the Constitution of the United States is hereby repealed.

Section 2.

The transportation or importation into any State, Territory, or possession of the United States for delivery or use therein of intoxicating liquors, in violation of the laws thereof, is hereby prohibited.

Section 3.

This article shall be inoperative unless it shall have been ratified as an amendment to the Constitution by conventions in the several States, as provided in the Constitution, within seven years from the date of the submission hereof to the States by the Congress.

AMENDMENT XXII

Passed by Congress March 21, 1947. Ratified February 27, 1951.

Section 1.

No person shall be elected to the office of the President more than twice, and no person who has held the office of President, or acted as President, for more than two years of a term to which some other person was elected President shall be elected to the office of the President more than once. But this Article shall not apply to any person holding the office of President when this Article was proposed by the Congress, and shall not prevent any person who may be holding the office of President, or acting as President, during the term within which this Article becomes operative from holding the office of President or acting as President during the remainder of such term.

Section 2.

This article shall be inoperative unless it shall have been ratified as an amendment to the Constitution by the legislatures of three-fourths of the several States within seven years from the date of its submission to the States by the Congress.

AMENDMENT XXIII

Passed by Congress June 16, 1960. Ratified March 29, 1961.

Section 1.

The District constituting the seat of Government of the United States shall appoint in such manner as the Congress may direct:

A number of electors of President and Vice President equal to the whole number of Senators and Representatives in Congress to which the District would be entitled if it were a State, but in no event more than the least populous State; they shall be in addition to those appointed by the States, but they shall be considered, for the purposes of the election of President and Vice President, to be electors appointed by a State; and they shall meet in the District and perform such duties as provided by the twelfth article of amendment.

Section 2.

The Congress shall have power to enforce this article by appropriate legislation.

AMENDMENT XXIV

Passed by Congress August 27, 1962. Ratified January 23, 1964.

Section 1.

The right of citizens of the United States to vote in any primary or other election for President or Vice President, for electors for President or Vice President, or for Senator or Representative in Congress, shall not be denied or abridged by the United States or any State by reason of failure to pay any poll tax or other tax.

Section 2.

The Congress shall have power to enforce this article by appropriate legislation.

AMENDMENT XXV

Passed by Congress July 6, 1965. Ratified February 10, 1967.

Note: Article II, section 1, of the Constitution was affected by the 25th amendment.

Section 1.

In case of the removal of the President from office or of his death or resignation, the Vice President shall become President.

Section 2.

Whenever there is a vacancy in the office of the Vice President, the President shall nominate a Vice President who shall take office upon confirmation by a majority vote of both Houses of Congress.

Section 3.

Whenever the President transmits to the President pro tempore of the Senate and the Speaker of the House of Representatives his written declaration that he is unable to discharge the powers and duties of his office, and until he transmits to them a written declaration to the contrary, such powers and duties shall be discharged by the Vice President as Acting President.

Section 4.

Whenever the Vice President and a majority of either the principal officers of the executive departments or of such other body as Congress may by law provide, transmit to the President pro tempore of the Senate and the Speaker of the House of Representatives their written declaration that the President is unable to discharge the powers and duties of his office, the Vice President shall immediately assume the powers and duties of the office as Acting President.

Thereafter, when the President transmits to the President pro tempore of the Senate and the Speaker of the House of Representatives his written declaration that no inability exists, he shall resume the powers and duties of his office unless the Vice President and a majority of either the principal officers of the executive department or of such other body as Congress may by law provide, transmit within four days to the President pro tempore of the Senate and the Speaker of the House of Representatives their written declaration that the President is unable to discharge the powers and duties of his office. Thereupon Congress shall decide the issue, assembling within forty-eight hours for that purpose if not in session. If the Congress, within twenty-one days after receipt of the latter written declaration, or, if Congress is not in session, within twenty-one days after Congress is required to assemble, determines by two-thirds vote of both Houses that the President is unable to discharge the powers and duties of his office, the Vice President shall continue to discharge the same as Acting President; otherwise, the President shall resume the powers and duties of his office.

AMENDMENT XXVI

Passed by Congress March 23, 1971. Ratified July 1, 1971.

Note: Amendment 14, section 2, of the Constitution was modified by section 1 of the 26th amendment.

Section 1.

The right of citizens of the United States, who are eighteen years of age or older, to vote shall not be denied or abridged by the United States or by any State on account of age.

Section 2.

The Congress shall have power to enforce this article by appropriate legislation.

AMENDMENT XXVII

Originally proposed Sept. 25, 1789. Ratified May 7, 1992.

No law, varying the compensation for the services of the Senators and Representatives, shall take effect, until an election of Representatives shall have intervened

States' Rights Under the U.S. Constitution

Selective incorporation under the 14th Amendment

The U.S. Constitution has Articles and Amendments that established constitutional rights.

The provisions in the Bill of Rights (i.e., the first ten Amendments to the Constitution) were initially binding upon only the federal government.

In time, most of these provisions became binding upon the states through *selective incorporation* into the *due process clause* of the 14th Amendment (i.e., reverse incorporation).

When a provision is made binding on a state, a state can no longer restrict the rights guaranteed in that provision.

The 1st Amendment guarantees the freedoms of speech, press, religion, and assembly.

The 5th Amendment protects the right to grand jury proceedings in federal criminal cases.

The 6th Amendment guarantees a right to confront witnesses (i.e., Confrontation Clause).

The right to confront witnesses was not *selectively incorporated* into the due process clause of the 14th Amendment and is not binding upon the states.

Therefore, persons involved in state criminal proceedings as a defendant have no federal constitutional right to grand jury proceedings.

Whether an individual has a right to a grand jury becomes a question of state law.

The 10th Amendment, which is part of the Bill of Rights, was ratified on December 15, 1791. It states the Constitution's principle of federalism by providing that powers not granted to the federal government by the Constitution, nor prohibited to the States, are reserved to the States or the people.

Federalism in the United States

Federalism in the United States is the evolving relationship between state governments and the federal government.

The American government has evolved from a system of dual federalism to associative federalism.

In "Federalist No. 46," James Madison wrote that the states and national government "are in fact but different agents and trustees of the people, constituted with different powers."

Alexander Hamilton, in "Federalist No. 28," suggested that both levels of government would exercise authority to the citizens' benefit: "If their [the peoples'] rights are invaded by either, they can make use of the other as the instrument of redress."[3]

Because the states were preexisting political entities, the U.S. Constitution did not need to define or explain federalism in one section, but it often mentions the rights and responsibilities of state governments and state officials in relation to the federal government.

The federal government has certain *express powers* (also called ***enumerated powers***), which are powers spelled out in the Constitution, including the right to levy taxes, declare war, and regulate interstate and foreign commerce.

Also, the *Necessary and Proper Clause* gives the federal government the *implied power* to pass any law "necessary and proper" to execute its express powers.

Enumerated powers of the Federal Government are contained in Article I, Section 8 of the U.S. Constitution.

Other powers—the *reserved powers*—are reserved to the people or the states under the 10th Amendment. The Supreme Court decision significantly expanded the power delegated to the federal government in *McCulloch v. Maryland* (1819) and the 13th, 14th and 15th, Amendments to the Constitution following the Civil War.

Law Essentials series

Constitutional Law

Contracts

Evidence

Real Property

Torts

Civil Procedure

Criminal Law and Criminal Procedure

Business Associations

Conflict of Laws

Family Law

Secured Transactions

Trusts and Estates

Visit our Amazon store

Comprehensive Glossary of Legal Terms

Over 2,100 essential legal terms defined and explained. An excellent reference source for law students, practitioners and readers seeking an understanding of legal vocabulary and its application.

Landmark U.S. Supreme Court Cases: Essential Summaries

Learn important constitutional cases that shaped American law. Understand how the evolving needs of society intersect with the U.S. Constitution. Short summaries of seminal Supreme Court cases focused on issues and holdings.

Visit our Amazon store

Frank J. Addivinola, Ph.D., J.D., L.LM., MBA

The lead author and chief editor of this preparation guide is Dr. Frank Addivinola. With his outstanding education, professional training, legal and business experience, and university teaching, Dr. Addivinola lent his expertise to develop this book.

Attorney Frank Addivinola is admitted to practice law in several jurisdictions. He has served as an academic advisor and mentor for students and practitioners.

Dr. Addivinola holds an undergraduate degree from Williams College. He completed his Masters at Harvard University, Masters in Biotechnology at Johns Hopkins University, Masters in Technology Management and MBA at the University of Maryland University College, J.D. and L.LM. from Suffolk University, and Ph.D. in Law and Public Policy from Northeastern University.

During his extensive teaching career, Dr. Addivinola taught university courses in Introduction to Law and developed law coursebooks. He received several awards for community service, research, and presentations.

Made in the USA
Las Vegas, NV
19 May 2024

90144179R00094